Builder's Essentials

Best Business Practices *for* Builders & Remodelers

Thomas N. Frisby

RS**Means**
CMDGROUP

Builder's Essentials

Best Business Practices
for
Builders &
Remodelers

*An
Easy-to-Use
Checklist
System*

Thomas N. Frisby

Copyright 2001

R.S. Means Company, Inc.
Construction Publishers & Consultants
Construction Plaza
63 Smiths Lane
Kingston, MA 02364-0800
(781) 585-7880

The editors of this book were Andrea Keenan and Howard Chandler. The managing editor was Mary Greene. The production manager was Michael Kokernak. The production coordinator was Marion Schofield. The electronic publishing specialist was Paula Reale-Camelio. The proofreader was Robin Richardson. The book and cover were designed by Norman R. Forgit.

Printed in the United States of America

10 9 8 7 6 5 4 3 2 1

Library of Congress Catalog Number Pending

ISBN 0-87629-619-3

Table of Contents

List of Checklists
and Illustrations

Checklists

List of Illustrations

Foreword

Some time ago, being a skilled builder ensured some measure of success. Today, the skilled builder must also be a skilled manager of the entire building process.

Today, more than ever, the builder's long-term success lies in customer satisfaction. Customers have access to the same information contractors have, and, as a result, may be more demanding. Roof leaks that were once resolved through callbacks, rework, and possibly exercising a manufacturer's warranty now have become the fuel of lawsuits.

Today's builder (whether single-family residential, multi-family, remodeling, or light commercial) must look for an "edge" over the competition through productivity improvement, effective use of software for estimating and budgeting, and maintaining a customer base. Computer technology and the Internet cannot and should not be ignored, and can make ordering supplies, getting work, or assisting customers easier and more efficient.

Today's builder is a strategic planner, a job planner, and a daily planner. He is a master of the fundamentals, overcoming problems, and finishing the job successfully.

Managing people better than your competitors gives you a definite advantage. Being able to attract and keep the best employees—both in the field and in the office—is a skill many builders do not have. Those builders who have honed this skill and are committed to solving labor shortages in their own companies are greatly improving their chances for success.

Cash flow management is the lifeblood of your company. Without it, the company shrivels and dies, or lives in continuous struggle. It is the measure of success and the chain that links all activities in your projects.

Cash flow management is the lifeblood of your company. Without it, the company shrivels and dies, or lives in continuous struggle. It is the measure of success and the chain that links all activities in your projects.

A company (large or small, new construction or remodeling) does three basic things: it *acquires* work, *performs* work, and *counts the money*. Ideally, a company does these things in a way that brings in profit and satisfies clients. This book will discuss each of these functions and provide checklists to help achieve these goals of profit and satisfaction.

A company should organize itself based on a sound plan and should stick to that plan in order to become profitable and stay profitable. There are three key requirements:

Purpose: To know (and communicate) the reasons why you are in business to your employees, customers, and the community. Your purpose may be to make a profit, but also to serve the community. What nobler purpose than to provide people with a home that brings them comfort and happiness—a quality home built with pride? When employees understand why you expect things to be done in a certain way, they are more apt to perform their work at a higher level.

People: To employ people who are above average or have the potential to be. Your job is to train, coach, evaluate, and motivate employees, provide them with a safe and superior work environment, and pay them fairly and reliably so that your company is the one they want to work for.

Process: Great companies have policies and processes—not for people to follow mindlessly, but to serve as guidelines to ensure a greater chance of success. These companies also have a concept of built-in-quality, which is an advantage over other companies.

The goal of this book is to make you successful—to get new builders and remodelers off on the right foot, and help experienced contractors put in practice in an organized way the principles they have learned. The checklists will serve as memory-joggers to help you plan and carry out the tasks you are responsible for, and to monitor the progress of these activities.

Note: Throughout this book, builders and remodelers are referred to in the masculine (he), though this should be understood by the reader to refer to both male and female genders.

Acknowledgments

The construction industry is one of the most challenging of the truly free enterprises in America. It has also been one of the highest risk and lowest profit industries. It has been my professional home for a third of a century, and has been very good to me. This book, aimed at improving the management practices of builders and remodelers, reducing their risks, and increasing their profits, is my own meager contribution to this great industry.

I would like to acknowledge the inspiration—for this and other endeavors—that continues to come from my children, Ryan and Erin Frisby. I would also like to acknowledge Mary Ashley Frisby.

The book's readability is due to the editing of Mary Greene, Andrea Keenan, and Howard Chandler.

— Thomas N. Frisby

About the Author and Contributors

Thomas Frisby, the author of this book, is the principal of The Frisby Group, LLC, a construction consulting firm based in Utah and South Carolina that does business nationwide. He is an attorney with an engineering, financial, and teaching background who has consulted with contractors across the nation. He specializes in assisting contractors to become more successful and profitable, and his management concepts are widely used. Mr. Frisby has taught courses including contract law and management, dispute resolution, strategic planning, and human resources management at the Texas A & M Construction Education Program and Clemson University Division of Building Science. He is the author of *How to Survive and Prosper in Construction*, also published by R.S. Means.

Howard Chandler, a contributor to and reviewer of this book, is a Senior Engineer/Editor at R.S. Means Company. He is the editor of Means' *Repair & Remodeling Cost Data* book and instructor for Means' estimating and project management seminars. Mr. Chandler has spent more than 25 years in the construction industry, as the owner of a residential construction company and manager of field operations for a firm specializing in commercial, industrial, and institutional construction. Mr. Chandler teaches construction estimating and project management at the Wentworth Institute of Technology. He has presented programs for the National Association of Home Builders (NAHB), and has conducted many seminars for builders at lumberyards and home centers throughout the U.S.

Wayne DelPico also reviewed and contributed to this book. He is Vice President of Construction for Bay State Contracting in Massachusetts, where he currently oversees public building construction projects. Mr. DelPico has over 20 years of experience in residential and commercial construction. He has a BS in Civil Engineering from Northeastern University in Boston, where he teaches construction estimating, scheduling, and project management courses. He is the author of *Plan Reading and Material Takeoff*, published by R.S. Means, and presents seminars on the same topic for Means.

How to Master Your Business with Checklists

Our Company:

☑ Has in place an organized process for managing our company.

☑ Has a process for making sure everyone knows what to do.

☑ Has a process for making sure everyone is doing what needs to be done.

☑ Works toward improving and streamlining current processes.

How to Master Your Business with Checklists

Thishis book is geared toward smaller-volume contractors who know their construction techniques—but who could benefit from some simple guidelines to improve their overall performance and profit. Few contractors dedicate the time needed to effectively manage their businesses, even though a few short hours could add so much in terms of profit and satisfaction. This means putting down the hammer or hanging up the phone once in a while and concentrating your efforts on making the business thrive. It means looking past today—right now, this job, this day— and envisioning a future to work toward, a goal to reach for.

Chances are, you already do many of the things discussed in this book, or have at least thought about them at one time or another. This book is not aimed at telling you what you have overlooked or have not done, but to help you improve what you already do, to help you take the bits and pieces and make them into a whole procedure for running a successful business.

The Importance of Good Management

Many builders go out of business after only a few years. They are overcome by the competition or their own weaknesses. The problem is that, while they may be excellent builders, they lack good business skills. They are very capable at installing materials, but they are not as good at establishing profitable contracts, and managing and performing the work required to fulfill those agreements. For long-term success, you must have expertise in carpentry and the types of construction your business offers. But you must also be a good project manager, contract manager, entrepreneur, marketer, logistics manager, decision-maker, information manager, financial manager, legal manager, and personnel manager (see Illustration 1.1).

A construction contractor must have more diverse skills than those required by almost any other industry.

Since building construction is a high-risk industry, successful contractors must also be good risk managers, as shown in Illustration 1.2. Some of these risks can and should be prevented. Others can be controlled. All must be *recognized* and *managed*. These same risks apply to large and small building and remodeling companies.

This book is written for those who *manage*, whether they manage a construction company as a whole or one aspect of the business, such as the actual construction, sales and marketing, or estimating. Managing means making a plan and creating a process for getting things done, gathering the needed resources, and then making sure it all happens as planned.

Every contractor must be a manager. You have to know the plan and execute it efficiently. You must identify the potential problems and figure out a way to deal with them while still making a profit. You have to continually figure out ways to make jobs more profitable while satisfying each customer.

The Contractor's Required Expertise

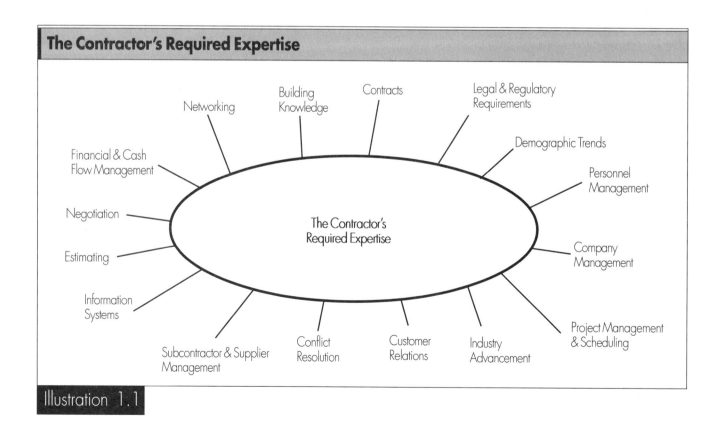

Illustration 1.1

Business and Financial Knowledge

Just because a person is the head of a construction company does not always mean that he is completely qualified for that role. Often someone who was a competent tradesperson or estimator starts his own business or climbs to the top of a company and takes on a leadership position. In many cases this person has no business or financial training.

A construction company, large or small, requires business management capability. It is rare in this day and age for a company to succeed without sound business and financial management practices. So, the checklist for the head of the company is a simple one-liner: "Am I the man for this job?" If the answer is "no" or "maybe," it is not too late to gather the basic knowledge that is required. This book gives you the chance to look at your skills objectively, recognize any weak areas, and make a plan to improve them.

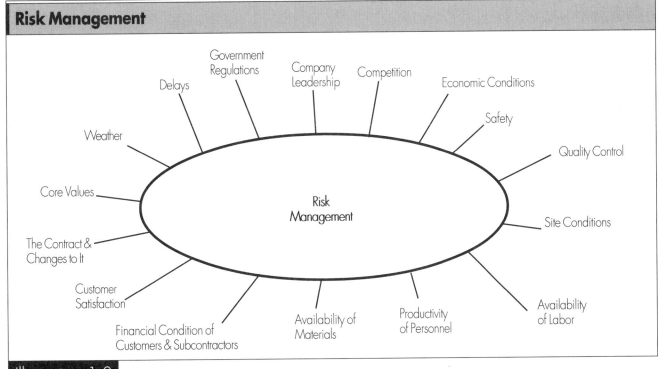

Risk Management

Government Regulations · Company Leadership · Competition · Economic Conditions · Delays · Safety · Weather · Quality Control · Core Values · Risk Management · Site Conditions · The Contract & Changes to It · Customer Satisfaction · Financial Condition of Customers & Subcontractors · Availability of Materials · Productivity of Personnel · Availability of Labor

Illustration 1.2

Leadership

Along with management is the need for leadership. Effective leaders have vision. They are continually looking ahead. They ask, where are we going, and how are we going to get there? How can we get better? What markets should we pursue? Leadership is what separates continually successful companies from those that don't reach their potential. Leaders don't just pull together labor when they're ready to start a job, but think ahead to upcoming labor shortages and ways to avoid the problem. Leadership involves making decisions like investing some of your profit in company growth, instead of buying a new boat or bigger house. Leadership involves staying informed about developments in the industry.

Managing Information

In the construction industry, information is the lifeblood of all decision-making, whether it helps you choose a new market to enter, which job to go after, how much of a contingency to include in the labor estimate for a risky job, or how to deal with changes under the contract. Information is crucial to every part of the construction process. Just consider the steps involved in a construction project, shown in Checklists 1 and 2. (Checklist 1 shows the basic steps; Checklist 2 breaks each step down into greater detail.)

Every step in the construction process is important, and often vital. Whether it's a two-day or a two-month job, each step must be thought out, planned, and properly executed. In some ways, smaller jobs have to be better planned and executed than larger ones; there just isn't enough money in them for delays or workmanship problems. Correct and complete information is directly linked to project success:

- With *accurate* information, you can make sound decisions and plan effectively.
- With *complete* information, you can make decisions without the fear of being "blind-sided" later on by unexpected developments.
- With *concise* information, you have time to give proper attention to all aspects of the job and business.
- With *timely* information, you can keep your momentum and not get sidetracked by unanswered questions.

Steps for Small Builders and Remodelers

Use this checklist to consider the basic tasks in getting and completing a job.
(See Checklist 2 for steps in more detail).

- ☐ Find a qualified customer.

- ☐ Develop a scope of work or plans.

- ☐ Develop an estimate.

- ☐ Make an agreement with the customer on scope, price, and schedule.

- ☐ Acquire permits.

- ☐ Develop a plan for completion.

- ☐ Organize:

    - ☐ Materials.

    - ☐ Tools and equipment.

    - ☐ Crews.

    - ☐ Subcontractors.

- ☐ Perform the work.

- ☐ Keep track of costs.

- ☐ Keep track of changes.

- ☐ Ensure quality work.

- ☐ Finish work on time.

- ☐ Conduct final inspection.

- ☐ Receive final payment.

Notes:

_____

_____

_____

_____

_____

_____

Checklist 1

7

Parts and Sub-Parts of a Construction Project

Use this checklist to make sure all the steps in your project are successfully completed.

☐ Review design/owner requirements.

☐ Clarify owner's budget limitations.

☐ Visit and investigate the site.

If new home construction:

   ☐ Conduct site search and site feasibility study (including environmental).

   ☐ Acquire land.

☐ Develop the project scope.

☐ Prepare drawings/sketches or check quality of plans and specifications prepared by others (architect).

☐ Prepare bid or price for owner. This involves:

   ☐ Clarifying owner-furnished equipment, materials, and services.

   ☐ Determining allowances.

   ☐ Doing quantity takeoffs.

   ☐ Getting supplier quotes/commitments on availability.

   ☐ Making preliminary plan and schedule.

   ☐ Evaluating risks and setting a contract price.

☐ You got the job. Present payment schedule and sign contract.

☐ Plan and schedule the project.

☐ Make financial arrangements such as:

   ☐ Insurance.

   ☐ Financing, if necessary.

☐ Pre-qualify subcontractors' ability and availability.

☐ Remediate site environmental problems, previously identified and priced.

☐ Obtain building permits.

☐ Order long lead-time materials and equipment.

☐ Obtain manufacturer information needed for installations.

☐ Notify approved subcontractors and confirm their participation and start dates.

☐ Plan your method to organize and track the project, such as a bar chart or other type of schedule.

Checklist 2

Parts and Sub-parts of a Construction Project *(continued)*

- ☐ On the job site, plan for:
  - ☐ Site access and parking.
  - ☐ Job site safety.
  - ☐ Toilet facilities.
  - ☐ Temporary utilities, if needed.
- ☐ Develop a plan for:
  - ☐ Material handling and storage.
  - ☐ Tools and equipment availability.
- ☐ Prepare the area for work.
- ☐ Set up workers, equipment, and materials at job site.
  - ☐ Plan and supervise daily activities.
  - ☐ Inform workers/subcontractors of tasks, methods, location, and duration.
  - ☐ Monitor safety measures.
  - ☐ Inspect work regularly to ensure quality.
  - ☐ Keep daily logs of work hours and equipment and materials used.
  - ☐ Review any change orders.
  - ☐ Work with inspectors to meet their requirements.

- ☐ Manage cash flow.
  - ☐ Keep track of invoices, billings, and payments.
  - ☐ Evaluate job progress versus schedule and payments.
- ☐ Note procedures needing improvement.
  - ☐ Clean up area and dispose of waste materials.
  - ☐ Remove, clean, and store reusable (temporary) materials and tools.
  - ☐ Clean and prepare site for finish landscaping (if applicable).
- ☐ Complete site work/landscaping.
- ☐ Move off site.
- ☐ Prepare and execute punch list.
- ☐ Get customer's agreement that project is complete.
- ☐ Provide owner with all manufacturer warranties, manuals, keys, etc.
- ☐ Transfer guarantee of construction/workmanship to customer.
- ☐ Obtain occupancy permit.
- ☐ Owner move-in.
- ☐ Receive final payment.
- ☐ Prepare invoices and pay bills.
- ☐ Promptly respond to any call-backs.

Checklist 2

Using Checklists to Steer Your Business to Success

How can you make sure that you give each step in your projects and your business the right attention? A proven system to keep track of key information and address the risks is *construction checklists*.

Construction Checklists

The pilot of a 747 or a Cessna 175 may have taken off and landed safely hundreds of times, yet he still uses multiple checklists each and every time to make sure that no crucial detail is overlooked. Managers in construction must also have a system to remember and follow through with the important details. No matter how large or small the company or project, there are certain fundamentals that must be taken care of if you are to be successful.

The checklists the pilot uses do not fly the plane—they simply remind the pilot of what he must do in order to fly it. The same is true of the construction checklists in this book. They alone will not manage a company, estimate a job, or build a project. But they will remind you to profitably manage the risks in a construction company or project.

The checklists in this chapter and all the chapters that follow have been proven in the industry through use by successful contractors. They can be photocopied and reused on future projects through years of business. You can also customize and print the electronic versions of the checklists by downloading them from the dedicated Web site: **http://www.rsmeans.com/supplement/busprac.html**

Use them year after year to improve your business.

Keep in mind that if the checklist system is to be effective, you must:

- Use the checklists routinely. Make them part of your current way of doing things, and refer to them for every project, no matter how big or small.

- Make sure the information you record on the checklists is concise, accurate, and relevant.

- If you have other management personnel, teach them how to use the checklists.

- Make sure that someone is accountable for the accuracy and completeness of the information recorded on the checklists. In the case of the 747, the mechanic must sign off on the repairs he has made and the equipment he has checked. It should be the same with data presented in your construction company.

- Tailor the checklists to your company. Each company is different, with unique ways of doing business. Since checklists include your procedures, they should be customized to fit your way of doing business. This is easy to do with the electronic versions of the checklists on the book's Web site.

- Do not use the checklists as substitutes for your own creative thinking and valuable experience. Use them as tools to make decision-making and management easier, more organized, and more effective.

What You Will Learn from This Book

The advice and checklists in this book are the result of years of construction experience, and will help you better manage your company. You will learn:

- The importance of properly managing the business end of the company.

- How to be a better manager—from improving your bookkeeping, to managing construction in the field, to handling people and doing a good job of planning.

- How to delevop and attain company goals—both short-term and long-term.

- How to create and maintain good business relationships with subs, customers, and your own personnel, as well as suppliers, the building department, and anyone else you deal with in your work.

- How to control quality and make sure that projects, personnel, and workmanship meet or exceed quality standards.

- How to successfully start and complete a project.

- Where to go for help (advisors, professional associations, publications, and computer software).

- How to stay out of trouble—legal and financial.

- How to handle some difficult situations that even the best builders can get into.

Strategic, Business, and Budget Planning

Our Company:

☑ Has a plan to maintain and grow the business.

☑ Understands that we need to make a profit.

☑ Manages the budget.

☑ Has an accounting plan (or reliable accountant).

☑ Has a plan for attracting and keeping employees.

☑ Listens to employees and customers.

☑ Has a value system that is followed by all employees.

☑ Uses appropriate computer technology.

☑ Has set aside funds for membership in professional trade associations.

Strategic, Business, and Budget Planning

S uccessful contractors plan for the future—both for the short- and long-term. The first plan to create is a *strategic plan*, sometimes called a *market plan*. The second is a *business plan*, which describes how your company will be organized so that it can put the strategic plan into action. The third plan is the *budget*, which is based on the first two.

Strategic Planning

Strategic planning identifies where you want to go, or your *destination*. The business plan is the *roadmap*, and the budget is the *fuel* for getting there. To develop a strategic plan, you should ask the following questions:

- What do we want our company to look like in three years?

- Do we want to grow and expand within three years (and if so, to what level?), or stay with the same volume of business?

- Do we want to be recognized leaders (whether remodeling, new home building, light commercial work, insurance repair, historic, or other specialty construction) in our local area?

- What are the best markets for us to be in (e.g., residential or commercial, new construction or remodeling)?

- What do we have to offer that would make potential customers choose us over competitors?

- Do we have a role model company that we want to emulate? ("We want to be just like…")

To generate a strategic plan, set aside some time to brainstorm your company's goals and write them down; then prioritize them. This is your strategic plan. Reevaluate the reality of these goals every few months by looking at how far your company has come at that point, and what needs to be done to hit the target. You may want to revise the plan along the way.

Without strategic planning, a company tends to react to the market, always trying to catch up with the competition. Successful companies plan for the future (and adjust as circumstances dictate). They are not "me, too" companies that simply follow what others are doing. Large or small, successful companies plan and know what they want for their future, and develop strategies and operations to make sure they reach their targets.

Talk with your employees, subcontractors, and suppliers about local construction methods and projects (as they are now, and coming trends). Discuss and plan with your own personnel what equipment you will need to invest in and what it will cost, and how to fulfill customers' needs. Use Checklist 3 to help you assess current market conditions and start developing your strategic plan.

Keeping up with the Market and Customer Needs

We know that market conditions and the economy change. A hot market for new homes and commercial space today can turn into a remodeling market in a matter of months. In strategic planning, you need to constantly look ahead to the next market conditions, changing needs of customers, new technologies, and the resources that you will need to stay ahead of the competition.

All legitimate contractors (those who are licensed, incorporated, registered, carry insurance, etc.) need to market their legitimacy to customers who may otherwise seek lower prices from part-timers on non-insured craftspeople. Whenever possible (in printed materials about your company, on your Web site, or in advertisements), reinforce your legitimacy, your experience, and your commitment to quality workmanship.

Strategic Planning

Use this checklist to determine your company's current condition.

The Market

What segments of the business have the most demand?

- ☐ Remodeling
- ☐ Kitchen & bath
- ☐ Additions
- ☐ New houses
- ☐ Light commercial projects (retail, office)
- ☐ Maintenance

What are the current market conditions?

- ☐ Interest rates (down/up)
- ☐ Inflation (down/up)
- ☐ Industry coming in (e.g., new mall, office complex, etc.)
- ☐ Industry going out (e.g., military base closures, retail stores going out of business, etc.)

What features are most in demand by the current market?

- ☐ Value
- ☐ High-end amenities
- ☐ Large space

Who is your primary competition? (Name companies and their specialties.)

_____

_____

_____

What do competitors offer to the market? (Strengths, services, type of construction)

_____

_____

_____

Customers

Who are your customers?

- ☐ Homeowners
- ☐ Developers
- ☐ Insurance company (repairs)

Required Expenses

How much money will be needed to prepare for this work?

For marketing _____

To generate cash flow for the project _____

For new tools and equipment _____

To hire new personnel _____

Checklist 3

17

Strategic Planning (continued)

Limitations

☐ The economy, customers' available income

☐ Labor shortage

☐ Material shortage

☐ Regulations (zoning, environmental, etc.)

☐ Your company's limited resources (available personnel)

☐ Limits on your ability to handle administrative tasks and accounting

☐ Limited available funds to invest in equipment, tools, trucks, etc.

☐ Limited resources for training employees

Sources of Information about the Market

☐ Local building departments

☐ Trade shows

☐ Lumberyards

☐ Publications such as *Builder* and *Professional Remodeler*

☐ Local chapters of trade groups such as NAHB, ABC, and NARI

☐ Local trade news

☐ Local and major newspapers

Notes:

_____

_____

_____

_____

Checklist 3

To identify the needs of your customers and then fulfill those needs, you must:

- Organize your resources (equipment, staff, expertise).
- Sell customers on your ability to perform.
- Perform profitably.
- Maintain enough profit and cash flow to be able to improve and invest in your company.

Customer Feedback

One source of information for a strategic plan is customer feedback—personal visits with customers to find out what kinds of construction projects they want or need. Surveying past and potential customers can help you decide what direction your business should take to meet customer expectations.

The Business Plan

The next step after strategic planning is to develop a plan for entering and capturing the market, to achieve the goals you have set forth. To create an effective business plan, you need to look at your current position and set a goal you can realistically shoot for. Then you can develop an action plan to make it happen.

Assessing Your Strengths and Weaknesses

You should begin with an honest and objective inventory of your strengths and weaknesses, or capabilities and limitations. This inventory is essential whether you are a two-person company or a firm with 50 employees, but it is especially important for small companies who cannot afford weaknesses; one or two big mistakes, and it's all over. The larger company often has enough assets to overcome problems, where a smaller one without a lot of resources cannot.

Use Checklists 4 and 5 to evaluate your company. With the results, you can then put together your strategic or business plan. Larger companies will develop a more detailed and extensive business plan, but the basic elements are the same for all companies.

Illustration 2.1 shows other points to remember when you are developing your plan.

Self-Inventory

Use this checklist to figure out where you are now and to set goals for improvement.

☐ You have a good reputation among customers, suppliers, and others in the community.

☐ Your customers are always satisfied.

☐ You train and develop employees and show that you value experience.

☐ You uphold strong values.

☐ You are a good business person. (You make a reasonable profit performing quality work.)

☐ You keep money in the company for growth.

☐ You are proactive about acquiring business.

☐ Rate your relationships, on a scale of 1-10, with:

a. Lending institutions _____

b. Subcontractors _____

c. Suppliers _____

d. Customers _____

e. Employees _____

List how your company is better than your competitiors.

a. _____

b. _____

c. _____

List the areas where your company is not as strong as your competitors.

a. _____

b. _____

c. _____

Rate your overall ability to maintain a steady flow of work.

a. _____

b. _____

c. _____

☐ Do you have adequate financial planning tools?

☐ Budget

☐ Accounting system

☐ Cash flow projection

☐ Labor cost reporting

☐ Job scheduling

Checklist 4

20

Strategic Plan Outline

Use this checklist to record your strategic plan.

☐ What type of construction do you plan to specialize in? *(e.g., finish work, kitchens and bathrooms, additions, new construction, etc.)* _____

☐ Our strengths that will give us a competitive advantage are: *(e.g., we do quality work, we return phone calls promptly, etc.)*

    a. _____

    _____

    b. _____

    _____

    c. _____

☐ Our plan to overcome our weaknesses include: *(e.g., inadequate tools means we need to budget for tool purchases, or too much wasted time means we need to manage our time better by arranging to have materials delivered instead of picking them up)*

    a. _____

    _____

    b. _____

    _____

    c. _____

    _____

☐ We want to increase our annual profits by this amount: _____

☐ To get there we will: *(e.g., buy materials at a better price, or get prices from three subs)*

_____

_____

_____

☐ Our marketing plan for reaching potential customers includes: *(e.g., advertising with truck lettering or starting a company Web site)*

_____

_____

_____

Our overall plan and related costs include:

    ☐ Start a new advertising program _____

    ☐ Get involved in the community *(such as local associations)* _____

    ☐ Hire another employee _____

    ☐ Purchase new tools and equipment _____

    ☐ Start a training program _____

    ☐ Improve safety procedures _____

Checklist 5

21

Developing a Business Plan

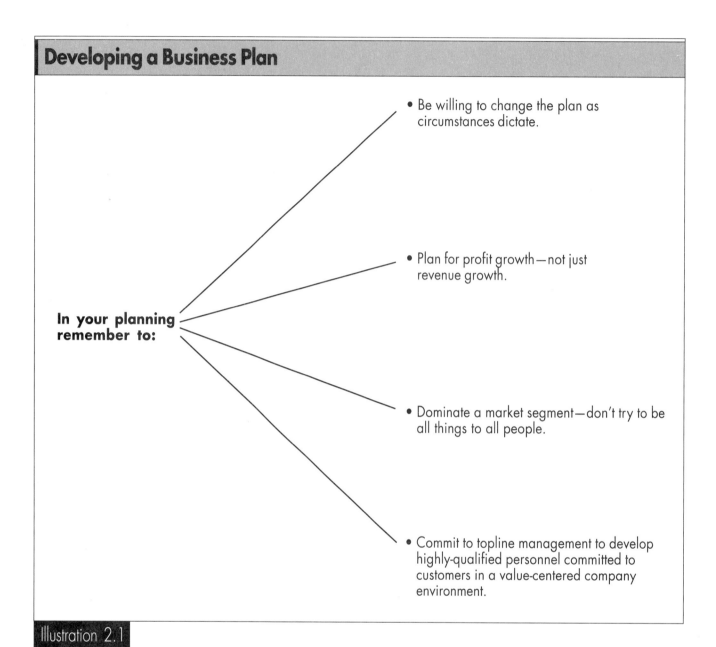

In your planning remember to:

- Be willing to change the plan as circumstances dictate.

- Plan for profit growth—not just revenue growth.

- Dominate a market segment—don't try to be all things to all people.

- Commit to topline management to develop highly-qualified personnel committed to customers in a value-centered company environment.

Illustration 2.1

Attracting and Retaining Top Personnel

During recent "boom times" in construction, labor has been tight. When creating strategic and business plans, consider the labor market and formulate a method to deal with a shortage of labor. Action you could take includes offering incentives (such as use of a company vehicle or other benefits like tickets to sports events or paid training or education) to your current personnel and treating them fairly so that they want to stay with your company. Providing safety equipment and the most current tools and equipment might be part of your plan. Most important is having the cash available to pay employees on a regular basis. *(See Chapter 3 for more on managing personnel.)*

Technology Planning

This is the New Economy, where technology drives the way we do business. To keep up with the competition, take care of current and future customers, improve productivity, *and* make a reasonable profit, you'll need to also keep up with computer technology. Successful contractors are always seeking new ways to get an "edge" on the competition. One of the most effective ways is using well-chosen technology to streamline the way you do your work. How are you doing with technology? Use Checklist 6 to check and to consider some items that you might want to include in your strategic and tactical plans.

Some or all of the items in Checklist 6 will apply to your business. Use technology to increase your productivity, make administrative and project management tasks easier and quicker, and attract and retain customers. Find out what kind of technology suits your goals and budget, then select and incorporate electronic tools and products that improve your productivity and/or make you more marketable.

Once you've purchased computer tools for business, provide the training necessary to make them work for your company. Set goals for personnel to come up to speed on new software, then reward them for their initiative.

A Word of Caution

The statement, "all change is not improvement, but all improvement involves change" applies to computer software you might purchase. All computer gadgetry is not necessarily improvement or cost-effective. For example, adding or changing an accounting software program could be disruptive and sometimes unnecessarily costly.

Are We in Step with Current Technology?

Check off what technology you currently use. In the space below, note what other items you might consider using in the future.

☐ Cell phones, laptop computers, or PDAs for field work

☐ Record-keeping software

☐ Estimating and cost control software

☐ Project management and scheduling software

☐ E-mail for time-saving communication

☐ E-commerce for convenience or cost advantages in material purchases

☐ Internet Web site to increase visibility to potential customers

☐ Internet advertising to recruit employees

☐ CAD software to produce drawings and show potential customers three-dimensional layouts

☐ Digital camera to document and monitor job progress

☐ Hi-tech features for projects such as energy management, audiovisual centers, and security systems

Notes:

_____

_____

_____

_____

_____

_____

_____

_____

_____

Checklist 6

24

Research and find the right computer technology that:

- Attracts customers, and
- Assists you in managing the business.

Here are some examples of useful computer applications.

Graphics

Most customers are impressed by technology. Many have a difficult time visualizing a finished space based on a drawing or sketch. More sophisticated graphics—with 3-D and color—can help customers see and even change the layout and functions of rooms to help them make decisions.

CAD

Computer-Assisted Drafting (CAD) is an excellent tool not only for your own use in planning a job, but also to help customers feel like participants in layout and design. Most architects and commercial and large-volume builders use CAD. Small-volume builders may find that CAD gives them an advantage over other competitors as a planning and customer-involvement tool. Builders who design and construct simply *must* have CAD and AutoCAD.

E-mail

E-mail is often the quickest way to leave an important message for someone—and to know that your message was received. Whether you use it to confirm a detail with customers or subcontractors, or to request information from suppliers, or even to submit or receive estimates or designs, e-mail is handy because it is cost-efficient, quick, and puts your thoughts in writing so that you have a record of the information you have exchanged. Some contractors even go as far as requiring that all subcontractors have e-mail so that communicating is easy and details are clear.

The Web

The Internet is a valuable marketing, communication, and project management tool. If you are involved in development or large projects, you are probably already an active Internet user. The Internet can be an important device for everything from getting product information to managing customers—from initial contact (perhaps through your own Web site) and throughout the project. Illustration 2.2 shows how you can use Web sites and the Internet to help run your company.

Web Site Technology

What It Is	What It Can Do
E-mail	Send messages and attachments (including images and video footage) to customers, subs, and others. Requests for proposals and bids can be delivered in a timely way and in a specified format for easy comparison.
Digital cameras	Take pictures of projects—before, during, and after—to check details with the building department or owner, or keep in your files, and to use to show potential customers your work.
Video cameras	Take video footage of projects. Can be used to show potential customers "tours" of the work you have done.
Internet	Allows you to research topics—from house plans, new products, industry news, and equipment, to professional trade associations and suppliers. If you have a Web site, customers can find out about your company when they search on the Internet.
Extranet	Can be used to host a Web site dedicated to one large project, such as a development or shopping center. Can include key information [schedules, RFIs (requests for information) logs, submittals, etc.] for architects, subs, suppliers, and customers to access.
Document Management	Web server can be the "filing cabinet" for documents, photos, and spreadsheets.

Notes:

_____

_____

_____

_____

_____

_____

Illustration 2.2

Web Referrals

More and more homeowners are turning to the Internet to locate qualified builders in their local areas. Many builder's associations, such as ABC and NARI, have Web sites with such referral programs, as do sites such as **http://www.contractor.com** and **http://improvenet.com**. Adding your company to some of these referral lists can be a valuable marketing tool and a good way to locate new customers in your area. Many of these services screen contractors ahead of time for licensing and customer satisfaction, which means that customers who do contact you will already have a sense of the kind of work that you do and your performance. Contractor.com's referral listings include over 800,000 contractors, and signing up may also qualify you for free Internet service, e-mail address, Web site, or other promotional savings. (See the "Resources" section of this book for contact information.)

Building Your Own Web Site

Many builders are setting up their own Web sites. This way, you can really show your customers your work—through descriptions of projects, photographs, and even video footage. The most successful sites create value for consumers, by letting them explore design options or linking them to other good sources of information. Your site could include a timeline of the steps in remodeling or building a home. Or, you might post other helpful information, such as tips for customers to maintain work done on their homes. If you do have a Web site or plan to put one together, you will need to keep it current by updating it regularly, and should make it as clear and straightforward as possible. Some tips for user-friendly Web site design include the following:

- Avoid lengthy descriptions. Use statements that are brief and to the point.

- Avoid large images that will take users too long to download.

- Avoid leading users to "dead ends." Always provide links back to your main page so that users don't have to backtrack.

- Avoid layouts that force users to scroll to access information.

- Advertise your Web site wherever you can—on your truck, on signs at your projects, and in brochures and other advertisements.

E-commerce

E-commerce—using the Internet to purchase goods—offers some interesting options for contractors. Large commercial contracting firms often shop for the best power rates on the Internet to offer financial incentives to customers. Residential builders and remodelers can find excellent Web sites for shopping on-line for house plans, kitchen and bath layouts, tools and equipment, building products, appliances, fixtures, specialty items, and furnishings. You can find detailed product information, compare prices, and place orders on the Internet. Some large home centers and lumberyards now take orders on-line for pick-up or delivery to a given location.

Depending on the size and type of project involved, material costs may run in the 30% or more range of the total project costs. Shopping on-line to find the most competitive prices and greatest availability of materials can give you a real advantage. Some contractors are even getting together to purchase materials in bulk. On-line auctions are a recent trend for getting good prices on construction items.

You can get an "edge" by using the Internet to work with customers. Let them know of good Web sites where they can select furniture and appliances that will suit the project. Many sites are interactive, allowing the customer to create a floor plan and insert products into it. NAHB and the contractor section of **http://www.contractor.com** can serve as good starting points for e-commerce links.

Mobile Devices

Hand-held devices such as cell phones, beepers, and portable digital assistants (PDAs) can provide you with a "mobile office." Many cell phone models can be linked to computers for e-mail and Internet access when hard-wired phones are not available. PDAs allow you to document project details while on the job site, saving time and reducing errors. You can write up punch lists, report expenses, communicate with your office and others, and deliver progress updates. You can also browse the Web and send and receive e-mail. Popular PDA models include Palm, Inc.'s PalmPilot, Handspring's Visor, and Microsoft's PocketPC. With such technology, you can control your project from any location.

Budget Planning

Construction companies must have the money to grow, to invest in technologies, to pay for the costs of the unexpected, and to cover the company's overhead when there is a slack month or two. Money used for these things is called *capital* or *investment*. Not having enough funds for these items is a key reason why contractors fail. Capital can come from savings, outside investors, a bank or outside lender, or from profits from the business. Builders often need money the most when they are unable to secure additional funds from an outside source and must rely on the profit from their projects. The business should be managed so that this profit money is available when needed. For this reason, the company's strategy to "keep profits in the company" to the extent reasonable is an extremely sound policy.

The profitable company aims for low overhead and high productivity. After the strategic and business planning is done, the results are presented in a budget, usually in the form of a spreadsheet. The budget describes the elements of your company's plan and assigns costs to them. For example, if your plan calls for developing a Web site, the overhead budget should include a line item for "Web site," and an estimate (budget) of its cost, including a time frame for when that cost is expected to be spent. The actual cost will be entered when the Web site is completed and paid for so that you can see the difference between what you planned to spend and what you actually spent.

Justifying Costs

There are two ways to develop the budget. One is to simply adjust last year's budget by a certain percentage, based on factors such as additional revenue from major projects, higher transportation costs, or added personnel. Begin each year by developing a budget based on your strategic and business planning sessions. The budget should be a detailed forecast of what it really takes to run the company and achieve your goals under current conditions. Every item on the budget should be justified, which means it is a clear necessity.

Direct and Overhead Costs

There are two categories of cost. The first is *direct* (often called "direct job costs"). These costs are related to field production and your employees, materials, tools, equipment, subcontractors, permits, and insurance. Direct costs must be priced project-to-project and must be completely captured in the contract price.

The second is *overhead costs*—the costs of running the home office (which may include a computer and office supplies, the company owner's time, and any accounting or administrative personnel or expenses). These costs are charged to the "overhead account." Many of these costs don't go up or down, no matter how much or little work you have. These costs are known as *fixed*, or *non-variable*, and include items such as mortgage payments. They must be paid whether or not you have revenue coming in. Some costs are considered *variable*, such as an estimator who works for you on a consulting basis and could be laid off in the event of a downturn.

Unnecessary overhead costs will weigh down your company, increase your interest charges, and often create an unnecessary debt-to-asset ratio. Overhead costs should be calculated as a percentage of direct job costs. The higher the percentage, the less competitive and less profitable your company.

Many companies treat direct costs for some items in the field—such as project managers, tools, and equipment—as overhead. The important thing is to make sure you capture *all* direct and overhead costs in your pricing. When the project is priced, you can apply an overhead percentage to the total direct cost figure. Someone must be accountable for those costs. If tools and equipment are priced as part of direct costs, and tracked to the job through the job cost budget, the job supervisor now has accountability for the tools and equipment budget. The result is usually more careful purchasing and maintenance of tools on the project. To be profitable, all elements of cost—direct or indirect—must be planned and monitored by a person who is responsible for the outcome.

Cash Flow Management

Cash flow is exactly that. It means running as much cash through the company as possible—and trying to make as much of it as possible remain in the company. Profitable companies try to always have cash available to pay their current bills. You should always be able to collect your receivables and pay what you owe. Liquid assets allow you to pay subcontractors and suppliers on time and maintain a solid financial reputation. This is a definite "edge." Justifying, keeping track of, and controlling overhead expenses helps you achieve this goal. Uncontrolled debt and heavy overhead expenses contribute to failure.

Debt

Debt can be the most destructive of all factors affecting cash flow. You can't just "lay it off" like you could an employee. Debt costs money (interest), which could be otherwise used to develop the company or add to profit.

The "One Year Rule"

For builders, some amount of carefully considered debt may be (and probably is) necessary—for the funds needed to purchase land and build a house, for example. This being the case, your company should always have enough money available to pay debt service (interest) on all of your indebtedness for a minimum of six months—and, ideally, one year—if there were suddenly a slowdown in business, or if a project were delayed.

Debt is only justified when it will clearly lead to profit. Is purchasing or leasing a new vehicle or renting or buying new office space going to make your company more efficient or bring in new, profitable business in clear, definable ways? Can you easily pass along the extra costs to new customers and revenue, or will the added overhead shrink your profit and be a millstone around your neck if times turn sour?

Many business people who are freewheeling financially have been very successful – for a while. But even while they are successful, profit is eroded, and so is liquidity. Liquidity is the contractor's lifeblood. To the banker, it is far more important than a new project coming up.

A word to the wise: Never get behind on federal or state taxes, or Social Security payments. Postpone other creditors in extreme circumstances, but never those.

Recession Planning

All companies should be prepared for the possibility of a slight-to-moderate downturn in the economy. Even if the downturn does not occur, being prepared financially makes your company stronger and better able to take advantage of new opportunities. Generally, as a company grows or takes on larger projects, its overhead grows, and the owner may take a less active role in the actual construction in order to pay more attention to the business side of the company. If the company is faced with rolling back or taking on smaller jobs than usual, the owner must be prepared to take jobs for less markup or even to return to the field more frequently. The key to recession planning is to recognize that temporary adjustments need to be made. Once you roll back, be prepared to grow again when the opportunity presents itself.

Accountability

To be truly effective, budget line items must be accounted for. For example, if there is someone in your company responsible for marketing efforts, that person should be held accountable for managing that budget and for its results. In a one-person company, that means treating the sales/marketing budget separately and making sure you manage it to achieve the planned results. This brings us to another point—all items in the overhead expense budget should be directly related to and measured against the company's success in acquiring profitable work, performing it profitably, and managing the company's money effectively.

Updating the Budget

When changes are made during the course of the year (such as hiring another employee), the extra expense should be justified, and the budget updated accordingly. Some of the budget items that tend to erode the business and that should be constantly screened and analyzed include the following:

- Insurance rates could mean high experience modification ratio (EMR), or poor safety performance. Your EMR is based on how many claims you have over a period of time. If you have no claims or very few, you will have a better rate.
- Interest could mean poor job or cash flow management.
- No discounts could mean poor cash flow management.
- Rework could mean errors in job interpretation or defects in construction.

Trends like these are "yellow flags" to take some affirmative action.

Revenue Budget

No matter the size of your company, you need to create a revenue budget—a *forecast* of your expected sales. This can be pretty tricky. Revenue forecasts take into consideration work that is already under contract or in progress, and what you (realistically) expect to acquire throughout the budget year. Revenue forecasts are broken down into two categories:

1. **Work in Process (WIP):** The balance to be completed on work already under contract (e.g., if you have a contract to build a house for $100,000 and have completed—and collected the payment for—50% of it, the forecasted revenue for that job for the coming year is $50,000).

2. **Anticipated Work:** Work that you anticipate will start during the current year and generate revenue. You can forecast anticipated work by considering:

   - *Your own recent experience* and the *trends* shown in your market studies.
   - *Potential work* already in the sales pipeline that you are confident will come through.
   - *Relationships* with people who may direct work your way, such as repair work for an insurance company you currently deal with.

When forecasting revenue, be conservative, even in hot markets. External events like weather, interest rate hikes, labor crunches, and shortages of supplies can interfere with your expected revenues.

The revenue budget will represent in dollars what your company has already formulated in your strategic plan. Budgets should never be only a financial exercise. They should be a product of a well-thought out game plan for acquiring and producing work. Of course, revenue doesn't just happen. Someone must be assigned the responsibility for making those sales.

Tracking the Budget

The budget should be used as a management tool for analyzing progress and making decisions. For example, in the first quarter of the year, a budget might show a plan similar to Illustration 2.3.

Now assume because of weather, the projects that you were supposed to start were delayed, as shown in Illustration 2.4. You can see that revenue is down, but you still have the same overhead. You must take action to keep the budget on track. You could do this with a big sales push to get more work later in the year, by reducing overhead, or both.

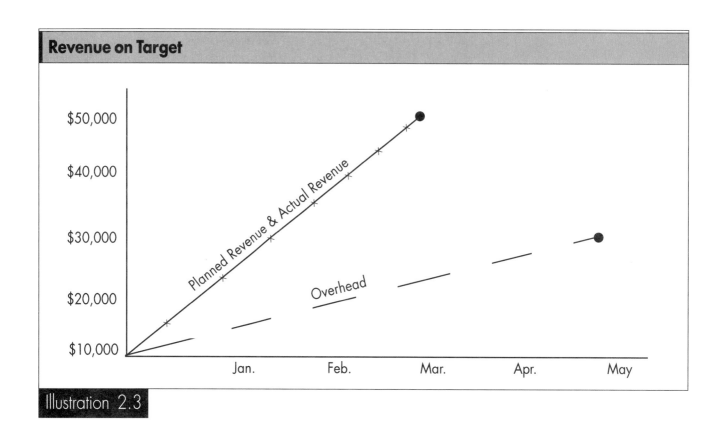

Illustration 2.3

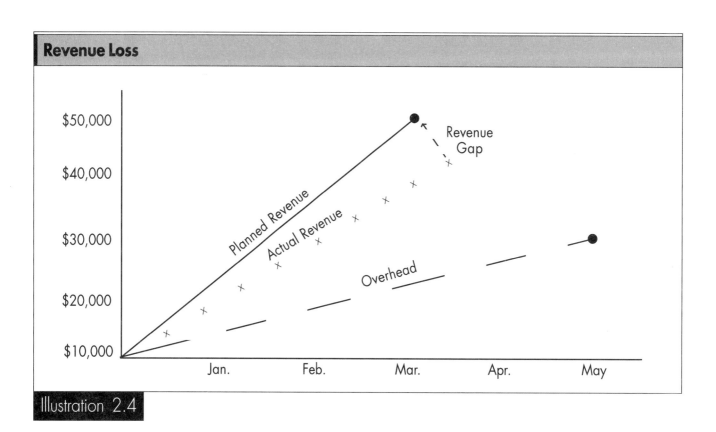

Illustration 2.4

But what if the reverse occurs, as in Illustration 2.5? Here sales are booming while overhead remains the same. Can the company handle it, or is this too much of a stretch for the current staff? It is time to look for additional resources.

Tracking the budget helps you understand how your company is doing according to your plan, what the trends are, and how to decide what actions should be taken to stay on track. The budget should be updated monthly to compare actual expenses and revenue with budget projections. Your monthly report is your "income statement," because it shows how much money you are making after all expenses have been paid.

Principles for Small-Volume Contractors

Illustration 2.6 shows how a budget could be set up for a small company.

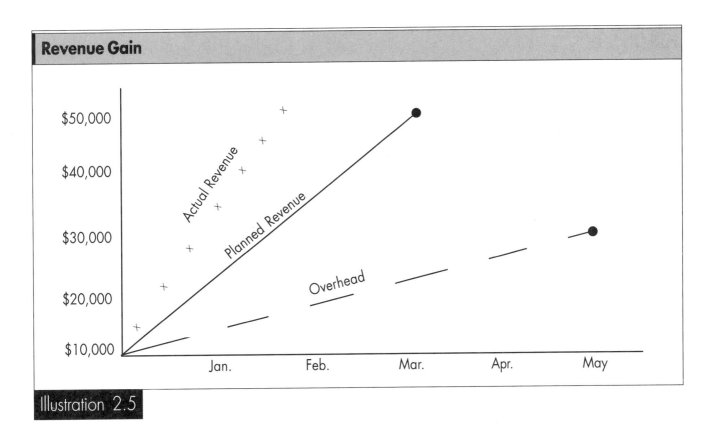

Revenue Gain

Illustration 2.5

35

Assume you can mark up the job cost of each project by 20%. If you can create a business that does $480,000 of total earned income for the year, you will have just about broken even if your direct job costs are $400,000 (with a 20% mark-up equal to $80,000, or just about enough to pay for your overhead expenses). If you bring in just $50,000 less in revenue, or one customer doesn't pay an invoice, or if unseasonable weather slows down your project, you are in trouble. If you want to expand and buy some needed equipment, there will be no available funds except by incurring debt. And if you are not meeting your budget, a bank may not be willing to extend a loan.

Accounting

To handle your accounting, you can either consult a reliable accountant, or implement computer software to help you. Any company, large or small, can use an off-the-shelf software program for performing budgeting functions. There are excellent software

Sample Budget

	Monthly	Annually
My salary	$4,000	$48,000
Pick-up trucks	1,000	12,000
Gas, oil, maintenance	500	6,000
Office rent	500	6,000
Office supplies	100	1,200
Telephone (including Internet server, cell, & pager)	500	6,000
Payroll taxes	300	3,600
Insurance liability	250	3,000
Medical insurance	550	6,600
Worker's compensation	300	3,600
Advertising	75	900
Tools/Expenditures	200	2,400
Total	$8,275	$99,300

Illustration 2.6

programs geared to small businesses including Quicken, Microsoft Money, Microsoft Office, Microsoft Project, Canon Office Ready, Peachtree Accounting, and ACCPAC Simply Accounting. (Microsoft Project also provides an excellent scheduling program.)

These software programs perform functions including:

- General ledger
- Balance sheet
- Income statement
- Cash flow projections
- Chart of accounts
- Customer reports
- Vendor reports
- Inventory reports
- Payroll reports

Whether you use an accountant or computer software, the success of your company relies on your ability to accurately forecast and control costs. Many construction companies fold because they do not understand the real costs of doing business, and focus too much of their attention on project management.

Accounting for a construction company involves the input, processing, and output of financial data. Each complete cycle is twelve months, with end-of-period processing at the close of each month and each year. Whatever system you use, it must be designed and operated properly, and must cover:

- Asset accounts (such as cash, equipment, and accounts receivable)
- Liability accounts (creditor's claims against your assets, such as accounts payable and withheld taxes)

What We Have Learned

The key to success in this business lies in planning by thinking ahead to realistic goals, forecasting revenue and required expenses, and making action plans to reach your goals. Strategic, business, and budget planning are sound business practices that help you stay on track. And once you have these processes in place and have been through a cycle or two over the first couple of years, it will seem like second nature to think of your business this way. Whether your company is big or small, you need to think about where you want to be, where you should be, and where you currently are. You need a budget to tell you how much revenue you will need and what profit margins you need. No bank will consider making an operational loan without a solid business plan and budget.

No matter how small or large the company is, it should be built in such a way that should you decide to go out of business someday, you can sell the business to a new owner, or step back and leave the day-to-day tasks to someone else. Successful small contractors recognize that their company is a business.

Chapter Three

Managing the Company

Our Company:

- ☑ Knows and practices proactive management principles.

- ☑ Establishes company policies and procedures.

- ☑ Manages cash flow in all company functions.

- ☑ Is committed to continual improvement of employees.

- ☑ Has good rapport among co-workers.

- ☑ Has low personnel turnover.

- ☑ Knows how to work effectively with clients (and architects).

- ☑ Is committed to building the team, including key subcontractors.

Managing the Company

Proactive management is constantly reducing your risks by watching out for hazards before they occur. Reactive management, on the other hand, is "putting out fires." While you can get insurance against forces beyond your control (such as weather damage), it's impossible to be insured for damage caused by bad management. The way to protect your company is to practice a proactive management style. Use Checklist 7 to see if your current management style is proactive, and to plan what you would like to do differently in the future. Research has shown that only a relatively few contractors manage to maintain a thriving business over the years. Those who do tend to have the traits shown in Checklist 7. See how your approach compares.

The Keys to Management

The owner of any construction company must manage productivity to ensure that *all* operations of the company perform as expected. This means paying close attention to "PPOIC," or:

People
Planning
Organization
Implementation
Control

It is important to give each of the five PPOIC items your conscious and deliberate attention. It is no accident that *people* are at the top of the list in PPOIC. While the products of the construction industry

Proactive Management

Use this checklist to help you attain a proactive management style.

☐ Know the business inside and out.

☐ Know the company's risks and how to manage them.

☐ Invest some of your profit to build the company.

☐ Set goals for the company.

☐ Look ahead, plan for the future, and foresee potential problems.

☐ Keep up with the times and new technology.

☐ Plan and schedule multiple jobs and tasks.

☐ Establish priorities at the beginning of each job.

☐ Monitor tasks to see that they are done correctly and on time.

☐ Make a commitment to improvement.

☐ Let others know what is expected from them.

☐ Demand quality performance.

☐ Instill a value system in employees and their work.

☐ Teach others by your own standards, examples, and coaching.

☐ Do not tolerate disloyalty, but do accept constructive discussion to reach decisions.

Notes:

_____

_____

_____

_____

_____

Checklist 7

are things, it is the people who commission, design, build, and pay for them. Use Checklist 8 to find out if you are meeting the essential requirements of PPOIC.

Expectations

As the head of the company, your job is to pull the entire organization together and make it function successfully through PPOIC. Once you have a market plan in place, you need to make sure the company is organized properly to acquire work, produce it profitably, and manage the risks successfully.

You and each of your employees must know what is expected, and what you, and they, can expect of others. Clarifying expectations is done by communicating what each person is to do and what each person can rely upon others to do. This is the central nervous system of a good organization, no matter what its size.

Unfortunately, this principle is not understood in many construction companies, which is one reason for so many failures. Use Checklist 9 to help you clarify your expectations of others, and to determine what you should expect from yourself.

Establishing Company Procedures

Creating a reliable system that all employees can count on is essential for success. It is also a way to avoid mistakes that interfere with your cash flow. The system does not need to be extensive (the checklists in this book provide a starting point), but should cover priority items, including:

- Contract review/scope of work (and knowing what to look for)
- Estimating
- Permitting
- Planning and scheduling
- Subcontractor selection and management
- Quality control
- Safety programs
- Project management
- Cost reporting
- Management of tools and equipment
- Personnel management

PPOIC Requirements

Use this checklist to make sure you address all aspects of PPOIC.

People

☐ Hire people who are qualified and properly trained for present and future jobs.

☐ Motivate people to get the work done—correctly and on time.

☐ Reward people for a job done well.

Planning

Identify the kind of work that will be most in demand and position your company so you are ready for it.

☐ Plan for markets.

☐ Plan for obtaining jobs.

☐ Plan for project scheduling.

☐ Plan for project delivery.

☐ Plan for financial management.

☐ Be prepared to deal with conflicts that come up.

Organize:

☐ Equipment and tools.

☐ Material handling.

Implementation

☐ Implement all plans and strategies. (Carry out what was planned and organized.)

Control

☐ Control all the steps of planning, organization, and implementation.

Checklist 8

Performance Expectations

Use this checklist to help make your expectations clear to everyone in your company, and to help clarify what you should expect of yourself.

☐ Give clear instructions to employees.

☐ Train employees.

☐ Review plans/specifications/drawings.

☐ Show employees and subs how they fit into the project schedule.

☐ Communicate your goals to the project team.

☐ Inform others (suppliers, inspectors) of the plan in a timely manner.

☐ Address tool and equipment needs.

☐ Create a material handling plan.

☐ Identify unusual conditions that will affect particular tasks.

☐ Plan for safety.

☐ Keep track of task durations.

☐ Insist on quality performance.

☐ Keep track of quality.

☐ Keep track of the budget.

☐ Keep track of labor hours and production goals.

☐ Keep track of how you would do the job better to meet budget goals, quality, and time.

☐ Listen to feedback from employees.

☐ Maintain good customer relationships.

Notes:

_____

_____

Checklist 9

Working Relationships on the Job

Strong leadership and management are essential to good working relationships. Leadership consists of establishing *what will be done*—the vision, the new markets, the new ways of doing things. Management is determining *how to do it* and making sure it gets done. But if leaders spend their time only managing, and managers spend their time only trying to lead, there will be conflicts and crises. In a one-person company, this means balancing your time and energy between leadership and management.

Good working relationships are not strained by arguments, or by having to correct mistakes. These situations don't occur if you think ahead and take action to prevent them. A great work atmosphere depends on great leadership and management. Let's look at some tests of how well you are doing using Checklists 10 and 11. Checklist 12 can be used to help ensure positive and productive working relationships.

In the construction business (in both sales and actual construction), the gold goes to the firm that can best manage relationships—not only with clients (who pay the bills), but with all the people (employees, suppliers, subs, architects, interior designers, and members of the building department) who enable your company to succeed. *(See Chapter 7 for more on subcontractor management.)*

Each employee must understand that effective relationships are a part of his job. You may have to work with some employees to teach them how to create and maintain effective relationships.

The first lesson in relationship-building is a simple little formula that is tried and true:

$$C + C + C = T$$

C = Competence
C = Character
C = Consistency
T = Trust

A number of studies show that successful projects and relationships are based on *trust*. You can build a business on it.

Successful Leadership

Successful leadership involves doing all of the following:

- ☐ Be in the right market niches.

- ☐ Create a market; don't wait for one to emerge.

- ☐ Get ahead of competitors.

- ☐ Motivate every level of your workforce.

- ☐ Have competent supervisors at every level.

- ☐ Instill company unity ("patriotism," "wear the jersey").

- ☐ Attract talented employees.

- ☐ Recognize and take opportunities for growth.

- ☐ Get involved with the community.

- ☐ Join appropriate trade associations to network and learn more about the industry.

- ☐ Know customer needs and have a strategy to fulfill them.

- ☐ Develop a company vision for the future.

Notes:

_____

_____

_____

_____

_____

_____

_____

Checklist 10

47

Successful Management

Successful management involves doing all of the following:

☐ Put in place sound policies and procedures, and make sure they are followed.

☐ Make sure the company has positive cash flow.

☐ Meet profit targets.

☐ Have effective methods to manage information.

☐ Maintain strong relationships with subcontractors and suppliers.

☐ Keep personnel turnover low.

☐ Have a percentage of repeat customers (customer satisfaction).

☐ Make judgments about the level of quality you will deliver.

☐ Follow through with sound plans.

☐ Manage conflict effectively.

☐ Use well-thought-out strategies to make the vision a reality.

☐ Minimize legal problems.

☐ Stay up-to-date on new technology and equipment.

☐ Participate in training programs and train employees.

Notes:

_____

_____

_____

_____

_____

Checklist 11

Successful Working Relationships

Successful working relationships result from all of the following:

- ☐ Input of ideas from all employees.
- ☐ Open communication.
- ☐ Fear-free, professional working atmosphere.
- ☐ Effective processes in place and used properly.
- ☐ Good communication between the job and the office.
- ☐ Strong value system.
- ☐ High standards.
- ☐ Reputation for integrity and quality work.
- ☐ Recognition of work done well.
- ☐ Good wages and benefits.
- ☐ Continual improvement (training).
- ☐ Opportunities for growth.
- ☐ Good tools (office and field).

Notes:

_____

_____

_____

_____

_____

_____

Checklist 12

Competence

There can be no trust without *competence*. There is no trust when the roof leaks, windowsills rot, or the basement slab heaves. There can be no trust when employees can't schedule the work well enough so that subs know things are ready for them when they arrive. There can be no trust when the punch lists are thicker than the original plans and specifications. Every member of the company should continue to learn new skills to maintain and improve their competence. This includes learning from your mistakes, and learning about advances in the industry that you can incorporate into your own business practices.

Competence also includes financial capacity. Perhaps you have lost money over the years because of defaulting subcontractors. This may happen when subs are in debt and unable to provide materials, and they may force you to take over the work when they are in trouble. A little checking in advance can often tip you off to this possibility. Contractors are wise to keep "an ear to the ground"—to keep up with competition and their subcontractors' financial health.

Character

The second "C" is for *character*. Though it's an old-fashioned word, it is revolutionizing the marketplace today. Customers expect to deal with *reliable* contractors and salespeople. When a sub says he will be on the job on a given date with given manpower, you want to be able to count on his being there. When you tell customers you will do something, they should be able to consider it done.

How often have you hired an employee out of desperation without thoroughly checking qualifications, only to lose time or money because of his incompetent performance or uncooperative, unreliable, or dishonest behavior? Remember, hiring is where it starts. Hiring is like the head of the river, and if you pollute that, you pollute everything downstream. The same can be said about customers—if you select one who is financially unstable or tries to take advantage of contractors, the cash flow downstream will also be polluted.

Consistency

The third "C" is for *consistency*—another way of showing what you do when the "rubber meets the road." If there is a warranty call due to a minor defect, the company may be quick to do the repair and swallow the cost. But what if the cost is significant—like finding out that all of the flashing was improperly installed, and the house is like a submarine with a screen door? Is the company willing to stand behind its promise, or does it try to duck?

Competence, character, and consistency together equal *trust*. Trust implies that you know how to run your business and that you can be counted on—always.

Trusting Customers

The contract plays a crucial role in your relationship with customers. It clearly explains what is expected of them and of you. Trust breaks down when the contract is not clear or the customer does not fully understand what he can expect from you. Discuss contract items with the customer. Review the scope of work, payment provisions, and how changes will be handled. Clarifying these points up-front can prevent a strained relationship—and serious problems—later on. *(See Chapter 4 for more on contracts.)*

In the world of building and remodeling, a reputation for trust practically ensures success or failure. With trust, you will gain references from satisfied clients that will build your business. Without trust, you're setting yourself up for failure.

Trust works both ways. Look out for yourself by avoiding customers who cannot provide the needed elements of trust. If you check your financial records over the years, you will probably find that some of your losses are from customers who could not afford to pay their bills or who tried to avoid paying for added scope. In many cases, a little checking ahead of time may have raised some warnings that these customers were high-risk. Talking to customers about your expectations for the payment schedule can help to determine their reliability. Your subcontractors and others in the community may have had dealings with certain customers, and may know if there is a likelihood of payment problems. Prudent contractors determine the risk and decide to either not accept the job, or to price and manage the risks. *(See Chapter 1 for more on the risks involved in construction projects.)*

Use Checklist 13 to deal with customers and to make sure that the relationship is built on trust.

Contractor/Customer Relationships

To maintain successful relationships with customers, you should do *all* of the following:

☐ Return calls and e-mails promptly (establish a company policy of doing so within a specified time frame, such as within 24 hours).

☐ Set aside time to thoroughly go over all aspects of the project with the customer—from the contract, to the schedule and payment, to what they should expect.

☐ Inform the customer of their obligations and rights.

☐ Keep the customer updated on the details and progress of the project.

☐ Provide the best quality possible for all projects, large or small.

☐ Give the customer relevant warranties and important product information and literature.

☐ Stay in touch with former customers.

Notes:

_____

_____

_____

_____

_____

_____

_____

_____

_____

_____

_____

_____

Checklist 13

Good Practices for Good Relationships

Following are some ways to ensure quality relationships with employees, subs, suppliers, and clients.

Give Recognition and Feedback

Recognition and *feedback* are important tools for managing all relationships. Your customer who is paying for the work loves feedback on progress. He wants to know that he is important, that his is the only project that your company is undertaking right now, and that all of your energy is focused on him. If problems occur, he doesn't want to be surprised—he wants to know about them and be able to count on you to make a plan to overcome them. Keep in mind that the customer has access to the same information you do. For example, never blame a delay on the building department or a sub when the owner can check in on his own!

Employees and subs also deserve to be informed about what is going on in the company, their own personal performance, and how close the company is to meeting its goals. A pat on the back and a word of encouragement are vital ingredients in relationship-building.

Understand the Other Person's Viewpoint

Relationships are often impaired because we simply to do not listen to others. Steven Covey (best-selling author of *Seven Habits of Highly Effective People*) says, "Seek first to understand." Before you tell the customer he is wrong, understand where he is coming from. Why does he feel as he does? Put yourself in his shoes. Before you jump on the architect, understand his position. What was the reason for specifying this product or material? By taking time to find out why the sub is not showing up, you might learn that he did, in fact, show up three previous times, but the project wasn't ready for him.

When the owner is screaming because the project is falling behind, find out the effect this delay if having on him. If the situation is urgent (such as if the owner has already sold his other house and must move into the new one by a given date), make every reasonable effort to meet his needs. If you can't possibly get all of the work done on time, do as much as possible in priority order—and stay in touch with the owner continuously about your progress.

The Golden Rule

Treat people in all your relationships as you would want to be treated yourself. If you are a builder, consider how you would feel if the house being built for you had an overrun schedule, a busted budget, a cracked slab, or a leaking roof, especially if you could never get a straight answer about what was going on. How would you want to be treated? That is how you treat your customer.

If you were an employee instead of the boss, how would you expect to be treated? With respect? Opportunity? Fair wages and incentives? Then that becomes your guiding light for how you manage the people you work with. Use Checklist 14 to review your overall management of personnel.

What We Have Learned

Neither successful nor unsuccessful companies just happen. Both are involved in an ongoing process of management. Managing a successful company means:

- Identifying and handling risks by being proactive.
- Having a solid organization built around PPOIC.
- Establishing and communicating your company procedures.
- Using leadership and sound management to create and maintain good working relationships.

The unsuccessful company just lets things happen instead of looking ahead and controlling events. The successful company looks ahead to the coming construction market, whereas the unsuccessful company reacts to it. The successful company manages risk, whereas the unsuccessful company gambles. The successful builder plans growth and grows moderately over the years, keeping his company strong by managing PPOIC. This includes looking for input from employees, training them, and communicating expectations to them. The unsuccessful builder hires personnel "off the street" and complains about bad working relationships and unreliability. The successful contractor plans how to organize the company and its projects, finances, and personnel development, whereas the unsuccessful contractor just deals with these issues as they come along.

The successful builder has a reliable plan for success, whereas the unsuccessful contractor leaps without thinking to take advantage of what seem like opportunities, without a strong organization.

Successful Personnel Management

Maintaining successful relationships with your employees involves doing all of the following:

- ☐ Recognize personnel (hiring, training, motivating, and rewarding) as a major responsibility. Treating your employees right can give you a definite edge over the competition. Look around you, and you will see that the best companies have the best employees!

- ☐ Develop a workplace environment that attracts and keeps good personnel. (This applies to both the office and the field.)

- ☐ Encourage experienced workers to help teach newcomers. This effort not only upgrades skills, but it also creates bonds and supports teamwork.

- ☐ Be the best of the best before expanding your business beyond your current capabilities.

- ☐ Manage subcontractors fairly, but competitively.

- ☐ Stay connected to the sources of job referrals in your community (e.g., realtors, subcontractors, architects, suppliers, local association chapters).

- ☐ Provide current tools and technology, both in the office and in the field, and the training to properly use them. Most employees, especially younger people, want to work for a company that offers modern tools of the trade—from computer technology to construction equipment. Provide small tools for employees to use.

- ☐ Establish and maintain a reputation for consistent, quality workmanship and well-planned jobs.

- ☐ Provide company work clothing such as caps, sweatshirts, hardhats, safety glasses, and other safety equipment.

Notes:

_____

_____

_____

_____

_____

Checklist 14

Staying Out of Trouble

Our Company:

☑ Stays up to date on legal and regulatory requirements.

☑ Reviews the scope of work and other contract provisions carefully with customers to avoid misunderstandings.

☑ Makes sure the scope of work described in the contract is the same as the scope of work that was estimated.

☑ Includes contract remedies for non-payment.

☑ Manages changes quickly and efficiently and documents them properly.

Chapter Four

Staying Out of Trouble

I n the construction industry, regulatory and legal requirements affect every activity—from contract interpretation and relationships with suppliers and personnel, through construction, and after the work is complete, as shown in Illustration 4.1. You should be familiar with all of these items as they relate to your business and professional relationships.

The best time to know the requirements is *before* you get into trouble. You should have an attorney available who can brief you on what is required, including lien laws in your jurisdiction. You should also have:

- **Copies of applicable building codes and standards** (such as the *International Building Code®* or *International Residential Code®* or your local requirements). You should also have information on licensing and post-construction claims if your state has statutes on these issues. *(See Chapter 6 for more on codes and standards.)*

- **Information from professional associations.** The National Association of Home Builders (NAHB), for example, offers publications on legal and regulatory issues, and also provides certification for builders in different specialties. Associations are also a good source for accurate information on safety requirements and for employee training. Be sure to make all employees aware of your requirements for safety on job sites. *(See Chapter 6 for more on training. See the "Resources" section for associations and contact information.)*

• **Updates from your insurance agent.** Have your agent brief you on the details of your coverage and potential for liability for situations that are not covered. This is especially important if your company is growing and you are taking on different kinds of work. For example, some equipment, such as large trucks and hoisting equipment, may require special operator licenses.

The Contract

Just about every transaction you are involved in is contractual. Small jobs, big jobs, and those in between are all governed by a contractual arrangement (formal or informal). Even a handshake can be a contract. Every contract has two distinct purposes: it is a management tool and a form of self-protection that safeguards your financial interests.

Many inexperienced builders start out trusting the word of the owner, not believing that they could get burned. These builders don't see the need for contracts, and believe that introducing them may discourage the customer. However, the contract should be viewed by

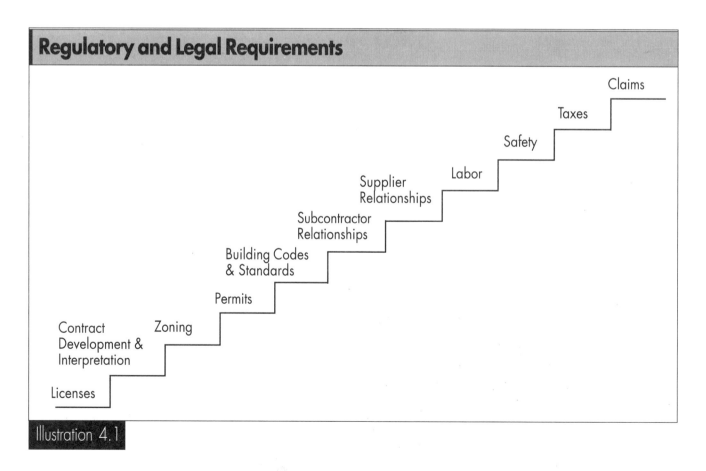

Regulatory and Legal Requirements

Claims

Taxes

Safety

Labor

Supplier Relationships

Subcontractor Relationships

Building Codes & Standards

Permits

Zoning

Contract Development & Interpretation

Licenses

Illustration 4.1

both parties as positive protection of *both* of their interests. The contract sets forth in a legally binding agreement the expectations each party has of the other.

On the most basic level, the contract must specify the following items:

- What is being built and when.
- The anticipated quality of the project.
- The cost of the project.
- How payments are to be made.
- How changes will be handled.
- What recourse a party has if the other doesn't fulfill their obligations.
- Warranties (implied or stated), and their terms.

Types of Contracts

Several types of contractual arrangements can be used for construction work. Choosing which type works best for your business means first assessing the risks involved with the work and your relationship with the customer. Following is a description of the most common forms of contracts and their advantages and disadvantages.

Lump Sum Contract

A lump contract specifies a total payment amount for your performance of the work. This is based on a defined scope of work—so, if you estimated correctly, you can reasonably expect that the work can be done for that amount. If the customer wants to add to or make changes to the specified work, then the total price may change based on the costs involved in making the change. A lump sum contract places the risk on you because you have to complete the work and meet the schedule as they are specified. Making a profit means having good estimating skills and being a good project manager.

Most customers prefer this arrangement because it pins down their exact financial obligation. "Progress payments" may be made on specified dates, or according to predetermined percentages of work completed. For small or short-term projects, one payment may be made at the end of the project.

If it is impossible to exactly quantify the work (such as in remodeling projects where there are a number of unknown conditions), you might use one of several other arrangements, such as unit prices or cost plus a fixed fee.

Unit Prices

You agree with the customer on a set price for each part of the work (for example, a unit price for each square foot of concrete flat work). You create a budget estimate that gives you both an idea of how much the total work will cost, knowing that it is impossible to pin down exact numbers and quantities. The final total will be based on the actual quantities of work required. Advantages: the customer has a guaranteed unit price for the work that has to be done, and you are protected because you don't have to guess at the quantities involved.

Cost Plus a Fixed Fee

If work is to begin before a definite scope of work is developed, or the work involves too many contingencies and unknowns to price it as a lump sum, you may consider using this type of contract. You agree with the customer about a general scope of work, and that you will be reimbursed for your actual costs plus a negotiated flat fee (which may be a fixed amount or a percentage of your costs). In some cases, there may be a cap or limit on the amount that can be spent without first getting the customer's approval.

If you use a cost plus fixed fee arrangement, be sure that:

- Your fee is enough for a reasonable profit and to cover your home office overhead.

- You agree with the customer on what costs will be recovered (some cost items may be excluded, such as home office overhead costs or re-work for negligently installed work).

- You keep accurate, detailed records of your actual costs. (Estimates of what you think something costs are not enough.)

- You can justify your expenses. (Getting a brother-in-law to do the plumbing when his price is higher than a competitor's cannot be justified.)

The advantage of cost plus fixed fee is that you don't have to include a large amount for contingencies that may not happen. You can also get the project moving sooner. On the other hand, you must keep careful and exact records in order to be paid. A possible disadvantage is that there can be delays while the owner and/or architect are making decisions for extra work—with little compensation for the inconvenience and lost opportunities this situation may cause you. The other negative is that customers may be reluctant to enter into this type of contract unless they know and trust you based on previous work you have done for them.

A variation of this arrangement is a *cost plus fee with not-to-exceed contract*, in which you guarantee that the project cost will not exceed a predetermined amount. Again, this system has distinct advantages to the owner because you have to assume the burden of cost control. This can be difficult if the owner is not flexible or willing to curb design or scope changes. However, it does provide you with a preset goal—a predetermined profit.

Labor Only

A labor-only contract pays you for your labor only. This type of contract may be used if the materials are furnished by the owner or others. To make a profit, you will have to mark up your labor charge more than you would in other types of contracts where you would have provided (and marked up) materials. You may also have to guarantee that you will be able to provide the labor needed to complete the job. For contractors with a limited number of employees, this can be difficult. The advantage of this type of contract is not having to procure materials, although this can be a drawback if the materials that are provided by the owner are damaged during installation. Extra materials may have to be purchased by the owner at additional cost.

Construction Management Fee Only

If you are overseeing the activities of subcontractors who are paid directly by the owner, you will want to enter into this type of agreement. You will be paid for the time you spend directing these subcontractors' activities, in addition to what you are paid for construction work.

Sources for Contracts

AIA documents, standard-form contracts published by the American Institute of Architects, can be purchased (or consulted if you prefer to write your own contract). [The AIA's Internet Web site (**http://www.e-architect.com**) contains information about purchasing contract documents, including a state-by-state list of distributors.] Keep in mind that AIA contract documents are developed and written by architects, and, as a result, they tend to favor the contractual position of the architect and his client, the owner. Other options are available, written for and by contractors and distributed by ABC (Associated Builders and Contractors), AGC (Association of General Contractors), and similar organizations. *(See the "Resources" section of this book for contact information.)* Illustration 4.2 is a sample contract that can be adjusted for your particular project and requirements.

The Contract as a Management Tool

In the first phase of a project, the contract is used as a management tool. It sets forth information that each party can use to manage their own functions, as well as the other party's functions. It defines the relationship between parties, and is the basis for determining what can be expected from whom. Checklist 15 includes items that should be clearly addressed in a thorough contract.

The goal of the project is to meet the requirements of the contract. Good, solid contract documents that convey a mutual understanding and an unconditional commitment to performance are the ingredients of a successful project, a satisfied customer, and longevity in the marketplace. Mutual understanding is the most important point for small builders and remodelers. All issues should be agreed on and understood by both parties. Changes may happen quickly, and decisions that don't seem very important at the time may turn into major disputes at the end of the project when bills are being resolved. Many builders tend not to think of these details as important, and may lose money unnecessarily to avoid conflict. As the builder, you are the construction professional leading the project, and as the leader, customers expect you to explain the contract and keep records of changes and decisions.

Scope of Work

The scope of work is one of the most important elements in the contract documents, because it represents the reason for the contract in the first place (i.e., what is being built). The scope of work should describe what each party will do, and when it will be done. If there are plans and specifications, they are a part of the scope of work. Checklist 16 will help you make sure that all necessary items are addressed in the scope of work.

The Schedule

The contract should include a schedule. Each party has responsibility to the schedule. You are responsible for maintaining the schedule by coordinating trades and providing adequate resources to accomplish the work described in the contract. The owner and architect (if there

Sample Contract

Work to be performed at: _____

Name: _____

Address: _____

Phone Number: _____

Date: _____

We hereby propose to furnish the materials and perform the necessary labor to complete the following work:

_____

_____

_____

_____

_____

_____

_____

_____

_____

In accordance with plans and specifications prepared by _____ dated _____ .
Specifically, sheets _____.

The above work is to be completed in a workmanlike manner in accordance with the drawings and specifications submitted for the above work for the sum of: _____

Payments are as follows: _____

_____

_____

Illustration 4.2

Sample Contract *(continued)*

Conditions of the Contract

1. Changes: No changes in the above work will be made without written authorization from the owner. Any alteration or deviation from the above work description involving extra cost or labor will be undertaken only after written order is signed by the contractor and the owner, and will be an extra charge in addition to the sum set forth in this contract. All agreements must be made in writing. The cost of changes to work or plans required by inspectors or governmental agencies, including special additional inspections (soil or water testing, engineering, etc.), is the responsibility of the owner.

2. Hidden Conditions: The contractor is not responsible for extra work resulting from hidden existing conditions that may be discovered during work. In the event that hazardous materials are discovered, necessary remediation work and costs are not included in this agreement. Any hidden conditions constituting a change in design or cost must be brought to the attention of the owner immediately. For changes, refer to paragraph 1 in Conditions of the Contract.

3. Schedule Delays: Project start and end dates are approximate, and may be affected by unforeseen conditions such as weather, material and equipment delays, and changes to the work. The schedule will be readjusted accordingly.

4. Non-Payment: If the scheduled payment is ____ days past due, the contractor reserves the right to stop work on the project within ____ days of written notice. The owner is responsible for all expenses related to non-payment, including reasonable legal fees, payment for work already performed, and other losses.

5. Site Safety: The contractor will make every effort to keep the work site safe, and is not responsible for injuries incurred by others on the site.

6. Dispute Resolution: In the event of a dispute that is not resolved between the contractor and owner, both parties agree to mediation prior to litigation as a term of this agreement.

7. Scope of Agreement: This contract reflects the entire agreement between the contractor and the owner, and takes precedence over any and all previous written or oral agreements.

Estimated Start Date: _____

Estimated Completion Date: _____

Company Name and Signature: _____ Date: _____

Owner Name and Signature: _____ Date: _____

Illustration 4.2

Essential Elements of the Contract

Use this checklist to make sure your contract addresses all of the key elements.

Scope of Work

☐ What is to be built? (No matter how small the job, a sketch is always valuable.)

☐ What is its size?

☐ What are its features?

☐ What is the quality level of materials and products?

☐ What are the expectations for finish appearance?

☐ When is it to be built? (Purchase and Sale agreements for new homes sometimes identify this.)

☐ Under what conditions may a contract be legitimately extended (adverse weather, for example) without penalty to you?

Schedule

☐ What is the schedule?

☐ Are there liquidated or actual damages?

☐ Are there excusable delays?

☐ Has this information been included in the subcontract agreements and purchase agreements?

☐ Does the customer have a timeline on his duties (financing, zoning, and so forth)?

Customer Duties

☐ Special access requirements.

☐ Design documents, if not provided by you.

☐ Financing in place.

☐ Owner-furnished equipment/materials to meet project schedule requirements.

☐ Owner-provided subcontractors/labor in accordance with project schedule.

☐ Other _____

Checklist 15

Essential Elements of the Contract *(continued)*

Role/Responsibilities of Other Parties

☐ The architect's responsibilities.

☐ The building department's responsibilities.

Changes

☐ How are changes made?

☐ Must the owner approve a change before the work is done?

☐ Must the owner approve your choice of materials or equipment manufacturers, etc.?

☐ What recourse is available if one party does not fulfill its obligations?

☐ Is mediation included as a step to resolve conflicts rather than litigation?

Payment

☐ What are the payment terms and conditions?

    ☐ Lump sum.

    ☐ Unit prices.

    ☐ Cost plus a fixed fee.

    ☐ Labor only.

    ☐ Construction management fee only.

☐ Are retainages to be withheld, and the basis of withholding clearly stated?

☐ Is timeliness of payments stated (e.g., "payable upon receipt" or "within seven days")?

☐ Are prerequisites stated for billings and final payments or withdrawals (e.g., from an escrow account)?

☐ Is lender's involvement clearly stated?

☐ Are lien release requirements stated?

Checklist 15

Essential Elements of the Contract *(continued)*

Deliverables

☐ What deliverables are required?

    ☐ Insurance certificates.

    ☐ Bonds.

    ☐ Lien releases.

    ☐ As-built plans necessary for any changes in site work, such as waterline, utilities, and septic generally required by the building department.

    ☐ Warranties, care, and operating instructions from vendors and subcontractors.

    ☐ Keys.

Notes:

_____

_____

_____

_____

_____

_____

_____

_____

_____

_____

_____

_____

Checklist 15

Scope of Work

Use this checklist to make sure your scope of work covers all the bases. The goal is to create a scope of work that is thorough enough that the client, after reviewing the documents, can say, "If it is built as described, I will be satisfied."

☐ You have reviewed the plans and specifications.

☐ The plans and specifications (or scope of work) are complete (and clear) except:

    ☐ Color selections to be made at a later date.

    ☐ Allowances.

    ☐ Owner-supplied materials or equipment (appliances, etc.).

    ☐ Other _____

☐ Unit prices you will charge for changed work are included (e.g., hourly cost for carpenter's extra time).

☐ The scope of work establishes:

    ☐ Quality requirements (e.g., grade of fixtures, dimensions, elevations).

    ☐ Responsibility for obtaining permits.

    ☐ Responsibility for other legal requirements (e.g., right of way).

    ☐ Responsibility for utility connections.

    ☐ Storage areas if provided by client.

    ☐ Landscaping plan.

    ☐ Protective covenants (e.g., restrictions on building elements related to historic districts, etc.).

☐ Environmental issues are clearly stated, including:

    ☐ Site protection.

    ☐ Remediation.

Checklist 16

Scope of Work *(continued)*

☐ Submittal requirements are stated (including time limits for processing).

☐ The performance schedule is stated.

☐ Any damages for failing to meet the schedule are clearly stated.

☐ Retainages are established.

☐ Clean-up and site protection provisions are included.

☐ Testing requirements are included.

☐ Inspection requirements are included.

☐ Roles are established, including:

    ☐ Client's role with regard to approvals and scope changes.

    ☐ Your role.

    ☐ Architect's role, including timeliness of decisions and authority to issue changes.

    ☐ Engineer's role.

    ☐ Interior designer's role.

    ☐ Landscape architect's role.

☐ Key risks are properly addressed, including:

    ☐ Water intrusion.

    ☐ Soil stability.

    ☐ Site drainage.

    ☐ Remediation of hazardous materials.

☐ Review by lender is addressed, if required.

Checklist 16

Scope of Work *(continued)*

☐ The conditions or requirements to begin work are established, including:

    ☐ Signed contract.

    ☐ Receipt of bond, if required.

    ☐ Insurance certificate.

    ☐ Permits required.

    ☐ Notices posted.

    ☐ Other _____

☐ As-built drawing requirements are addressed in the contract.

☐ Payment schedule and provisions are addressed in the contract.

☐ Mediation provisions are addressed in the contract.

Notes:

_____

_____

_____

_____

_____

_____

_____

_____

_____

_____

Checklist 16

is one) also have responsibilities toward maintaining the schedule. These include answering requests for information, reviewing and approving product materials and samples in a timely manner, selecting colors and products, coordinating owner-supplied materials and products, and, most importantly, approving and paying on time. Nothing can slow the progress of a project like an owner who is reluctant to pay the bill.

The schedule is an essential management tool used to:

- Plan work for you, the architect, subcontractors, suppliers, and inspectors.

- Measure progress as a basis for payments.

- Look ahead to identify potential problems and take action to prevent them.

- Identify nonperformance problems.

For these reasons, it is important to address the schedule in the contract documents. The schedule should require all of the items in Checklist 17. *(See Chapter 5 for more on scheduling and job site planning.)*

Liquidated and Actual Damages

On larger projects, the contract may be prepared by the owner's representative (such as the architect) and may in some cases include provisions for liquidated or actual damages if there is a chance the client may suffer financial loss if the project is not completed on time. If there is such a provision, the amount of damages should be:

- Reasonable in amount

- Not a penalty

- Related to expenses such as:

    — Additional time required from the architect.

    — Lodging or furniture storage fees and extra transportation costs.

    — Delay of occupancy.

Any contract that contains a damages or penalty clause for failing to meet the schedule has serious legal consequences and should not be taken lightly. It is often advisable to have an attorney review and comment on the contract before signing it. Spending a few dollars up-front may save you from spending a lot more on legal fees later on.

Schedule Requirements for the Contract

Use this checklist to make sure the contract addresses these schedule requirements.

☐ The schedule (whether a simple bar graph or a more sophisticated format) has been created.

☐ The schedule has been submitted to the client (and the architect if one is involved) for review at the beginning of the project, and you have their agreement on it.

The schedule clearly states:

    ☐ Client approvals and time limits for decision-making.

    ☐ Inspection events.

☐ The schedule will be updated when necessary.

☐ Each pay request includes a schedule reflecting progress through that billing cycle.

Notes:

_____

_____

_____

_____

_____

_____

_____

_____

_____

_____

_____

Checklist 17

Excusable Delays

The contract should include a provision that protects you from damages caused by schedule delays *beyond your control*, such as the client's changes or unforeseeable weather. Labor and material shortages do *not* excuse performance, except when shortages are beyond your control (such as if drywall is not available, fixtures are out of stock, or transportation strikes interfere with delivery). To protect yourself and your relationship with your customer, you must keep him informed and document these communications.

Changes

Changes to the project should be avoided whenever possible and handled quickly if they do occur. The most damaging changes occur at distinct time intervals for any of a number of reasons, and usually result in work delays. Use Checklist 18 at the beginning of each project to assess your risk for delays. Use Checklist 19 to identify what effects changes will have on your project.

For the most part, changes can be avoided or at least effectively managed if:

- All parties identify them as potential problems at the outset of the project.

- All parties commit to avoiding them and effectively manage them using a stated method if they do arise.

- Unit prices for changed work are included in your proposal and the contract.

- The owner (and the architect) have established time limits for decision-making in the contract documents.

There are several versions of change clauses. The *bilateral change clause* requires both parties to agree on a change (including price) *before* any work begins on the change. This method can resolve any disputes up-front before time and money have been spent, provided that the parties are able to reach an agreement.

The *unilateral change clause* gives the owner the sole right to order a change even if the parties do not agree on whose responsibility it is or on the price. This clause keeps progress going, and forces you to keep detailed records of your actual costs.

Finally, the *construction change directive*, which is now incorporated in AIA contract documents, permits the client to direct you to do the work and includes the client's estimate of the work. You can dispute the estimate, but again must keep detailed records of actual costs

Assessing Your Risk for Delays

Use this checklist to identify items that could result in delays.

At the front end of the project:

☐ Site conditions not adequately addressed in the design phase.

☐ Permitting, right-of-way, or easement delays.

☐ Delays in processing required submittals.

☐ Color, product, and material selections.

During the project:

☐ Client or architect changing their minds or delaying decisions.

☐ Conflicts or discrepancies in dimensions or elevation.

At the end of the project:

☐ Dispute over quality.

Notes:

_____

_____

_____

_____

_____

_____

_____

_____

_____

_____

Checklist 18

Reacting to Project Changes

Use this checklist to determine what effects changes have on your project.

☐ Add to the scope of work.

☐ Delay work activities while waiting for decisions.

☐ Delay the project completion date because it may take longer to perform the work.

☐ Increase costs due to overtime to try to meet the schedule.

☐ Increase costs due to additional or more costly materials.

☐ Delay the work into a different season where weather conditions or temperatures will make certain construction operations more difficult and costly.

☐ Delay subsequent projects that you have lined up.

Notes:

_____

_____

_____

_____

_____

_____

_____

_____

_____

_____

_____

_____

Checklist 19

incurred on the work that you contend is outside of your original scope. This includes keeping track of extra costs for labor, material, equipment, and tools related to the change.

Of course, once there is a plan, it is likely to change. The scope of work, if it is a thorough, clear statement of work understood by all up-front, is the best guardian against changes to the contract documents. The contract should clearly specify who has the authority to order changes. You must be certain to take instructions from that person to proceed with changed work. Often, the architect does not have this authority; it is important to clarify this issue at the beginning.

Payment

The contract is a *cash flow* tool. If you perform properly on schedule, the cash comes in. If you protect yourself from the possibility that the customer will not pay, the cash comes in. If not, cash flow problems result, which affect your profitability and ability to stay in business.

Ask any builder (or subcontractor or supplier) what the most important thing is that a client can do to attract good contractors who will go the extra mile to build in quality and meet the schedule, and the answer will be *prompt payment*. The contract should be clear about payment terms and conditions. It should also specify the role of the lender (if there is one) in the approval process. For example, the lender (bank, mortgage company, or credit union) may have to approve changes or review the progress of the work. These issues should be addressed in the contract documents. Subcontractors also need to understand up-front how the lender's payment schedule will affect payment for their part of the work.

Withholding Payment

The allowable reasons for withholding payment are set forth in standard documents, such as those published by the AIA. In addition, the statement of work in the contract may specify events that carry a withholding stipulation, such as:

- Failure to process submittals on time.
- Failure to meet certain critical milestone dates, such as completion of the foundation or dry-in/weather-tight.

If the owner withholds money, he must provide documentation that supports his position.

A Contractor's Remedies

Believe it or not, it is not the fine print that creates litigation. Disputes are created by:

- Unclear scopes of work, or

- Lack of accountability or performance by one of the parties.

However, a good contract gives each party *remedies* for breach of contract against the defaulting party. But there is a bit of a catch. Normally, for one party to have a remedy against another party, his hands must be clean, too (called the "clean hands doctrine"). For example:

- If the customer hasn't paid on time, you must be able to show that you have provided quality workmanship, on schedule, in order to collect.

- If you are claiming an extra, you must show that you have provided the written notification required by the contract.

Dealing with Conflict

Even in the best of relationships, conflicts do occur. Conflicts—whether between you and the customer, or you and an employee—can change a good relationship into a battleground. How you handle conflicts is one of the keys to success (or failure). There are two types of conflicts: *content* and *relationship*. Here are a couple of examples:

Content Conflicts: The owner is upset by the number of knots in the exterior trim and suggests that the contractor is cutting corners. This conflict relates to the scope of work and the expectations of each party. This situation could be resolved by explaining to the owner that the material used is industry-standard, and that premium, knot-free material would have increased the cost; that the final, treated and painted surface will not show the knots; and that changing the trim already installed would be costly and delay the job. If this does not help resolve the conflict, an unbiased third party could review the dispute and provide an opinion.

Relationship Conflicts: The above content conflict can quickly degrade into a relationship conflict if the builder or owner begins attacking people and not issues. The customer may say something like, "There you go, trying to beat me out of something. That's how contractors are these days." The builder retaliates, "What do you mean—you've been trying to get something for nothing ever since this project began!" Once the relationship suffers, it's that much harder to solve the "content" issue.

The same problem exists with subs: "You lied to me again about when you were coming to the job," or in-house employees: "I just don't know what is wrong with you—you'll never catch on," or with the architect: "That's the worst set of plans I've ever seen."

Relationship conflicts cost money, lose customers, and damage your reputation. They are not consistent with profit and should be avoided.

Mediation

Most remedies, such as *arbitration* and *litigation*, are quite expensive, requiring substantial fees, time, and an imposed verdict. Many contracts today require *mediation* as a remedy prior to instituting arbitration or other legal action. (AIA documents include such provisions.) A *mediator* is an objective third party (sometimes named in the contract) whose job it is to quickly help the parties negotiate their differences without resorting to arbitration or litigation. The parties involved must come to an agreement themselves, with the help of the mediator, rather than being told how the issue will be resolved.

For smaller businesses especially, and for clients who are not wealthy, mediation is often an effective and inexpensive solution. Not only do you both save time and money (mediation can actually take place at the job site, and without court fees), but you may be able to solve a disagreement without sacrificing your professional relationship.

The contract should outline the terms of mediation in case a conflict arises. The contract should include a statement about requiring all involved parties to be part of the mediation, including subcontractors and the architect, for example.

A Contractor's Rights

In addition to mediation, you should include the following remedies in the contract:

- The right to *file a lien* for non-payment for materials or labor.
- The right to *suspend work* if the customer does not (unjustifiably) pay within 10-15 days.
- The right to *claim interest* for late payments.

- The right to *claim reasonable attorney's fees* if collection measures are instituted.

- The right to *claim damages for delay* if your schedule is delayed due to acts of the customer (or the customer's architect).

These remedies may sound harsh to some, and smaller contractors might shy away from mentioning terms like "lien" and "attorney." However, the astute builder understands that these should be last resort measures, and while they need to be stated in the contract to protect the builder, they should never be used as threats.

Documentation

The customer has remedies that, in many states, go beyond those specified in the contract (again, check with an attorney). Some customers who claim deficiencies in construction bring lawsuits against the builder. [If more than two homes, for example, in a development, this is a *class action lawsuit*. Often, these lawsuits are filed many years after construction (within the time limits of state statutes).] How can you protect yourself? The best possible advice is to *do it right the first time, and document that it was done right.*

While no one expects problems of this sort, you need to be prepared in the event that something happens. For example, what if a siding project fails after ten years? What is your obligation?

You should maintain files for at least five years that contain all of the items listed in Checklist 20 for each project. This is one of the best pieces of advice for builders and remodelers. Documentation is to the construction industry what location is to the real estate industry—it can break your company if you don't have it. The importance of accurate and thorough documentation cannot be understated. Done correctly, it can be the best deterrent against litigation, and a tool for conflict resolution.

It is particularly important to document all *communication, agreements, changes,* and *amendments* in writing. The problem with a handshake agreement or a claim of "we trust each other" is that the hand has very little memory. If the work to be performed is put in writing, the expectations of both parties are clear so there are no uncertainties later on.

Document Everything for Five Years

Use this checklist to make sure you keep files of important job documents.

☐ The contract and all changes.

☐ The plans and specifications.

☐ All supply contracts.

☐ All subcontracts (and correspondence).

☐ All building inspection reports and your own quality checklists *(see also final inspection report in Chapter 6)*.

☐ Photographs documenting unforeseen conditions and critical installations, such as structural framing, electrical, and rough plumbing.

☐ Building layout and as-built drawings.

☐ All communication (letters, e-mail, invoices, etc.), agreements, and documented project changes.

Notes:

_____

_____

_____

_____

_____

_____

_____

_____

_____

_____

_____

Checklist 20

Manufacturer's Recommendations

Builders are sometimes sued because of defective materials or products, but more often it's a case of payment being withheld because of these kinds of quality issues. It is your responsibility to make sure the material has been installed in accordance with the manufacturer's recommendations. If a claim is made that your material/product/installation is defective, and you have followed the manufacturer's recommendations, then you should immediately put the manufacturer on notice. If a claim is filed, contact your attorney and insurance carrier (if you have liability coverage that might apply to this type of situation). *(See the "Crisis Control" section at the back of the book for more on this topic.)*

What We Have Learned

All of the issues covered in this chapter are critical to the success of any builder or remodeler. Contractor desk sales representatives indicate that many of their customers are good builders or tradespeople, but poor business people. Builders with good business skills know how to document and manage their projects using proper and timely communications. The successful contractor understands the difference between his money and what needs to be set aside for subcontractors, suppliers, lending institutions, and government agencies. He knows how to track the actual cost of the project at any given time and how to create profitable, quality jobs. How is this done? By either consciously or subconsciously applying the points made in this chapter. You will stay out of trouble and be more successful.

Job Set-Up and Planning

Our Company:

☑ Is committed to planning and scheduling.

☑ Has and follows a planning process.

☑ Does a good job:

  ☑ Estimating project costs.

  ☑ Budgeting project expenses.

  ☑ Tracking material, labor, and equipment costs.

  ☑ Tracking total costs of all jobs.

  ☑ Handling changes.

  ☑ Scheduling projects.

  ☑ Providing quality workmanship.

☑ Has an early warning system to alert us to job-related problems.

Job Set-Up and Planning

Planning is what needs to be done at the outset of a project. Often builders begin a project before fully reading the plans and specifications or taking the time to become familiar with the estimate. In other words, they begin work before they begin to plan. Before long, in the midst of all the activity, it's not surprising that one or more items falls through the cracks.

The management of a construction project involves several important tasks, including:

- Figuring out what needs to be done (*planning*).

- Deciding when it needs to be done (*scheduling*).

- Doing what needs to be done according to the schedule (*implementation*).

- Correcting problems when things don't go according to the schedule.

A successful project is well planned. A three-day remodel of a bathroom requires proper planning of the crew (including work and materials provided by subcontractors and suppliers) followed by execution of that plan if you are to make money. Productivity and profit are directly affected by planning.

The First 25%

Experience shows that the first 25% of a job is the most important. If the job is kicked off well, the rest has a much better chance of running smoothly. Up-front planning includes:

- Putting an effective schedule in place (coordinated with all parties).

- Getting material and product approvals, owner/architect decisions made.
- Mobilizing crews.
- Ordering materials and equipment.
- Identifying and managing priorities.
- Establishing momentum; setting a pace and motivating workers.

All too often, builders under-manage the beginning of a project, and then have to intensify management as crises (that were preventable) occur. One of the reasons for this failure to plan is that many builders emphasize the acquisition of work ("I've got to have that job"), but then skimp on the project management. Another reason for failure to plan is that many contractors (and their field staff) simply are not aware of all the facets of good planning. Nor do they fully realize the cost-benefit ratio of effective planning.

Illustration 5.1 shows how projects that are properly planned from the start and throughout can lead to a labor unit cost that is equal to or better than the bid cost. Projects that are underplanned have a tendency to result in labor cost overruns.

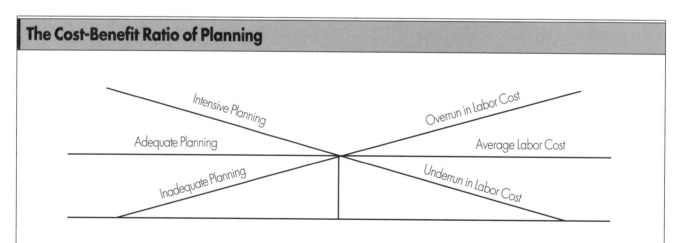

The Cost-Benefit Ratio of Planning

This illustration shows how projects that are well planned at the outset, and *continuously* planned throughout the job, generally result in a labor unit cost equal to or better than the bid cost. It also shows that in general, underplanned and uncontrolled projects produce labor costs overruns.

Illustration 5.1

Planning is a management function, not a clerical or administrative task. It involves:

- Deciding *what* is to be done.
- Deciding *who* is to do it.
- Deciding *how* it is to be done.
- Understanding and managing the *financial risks* as established by the contract documents (i.e., effective contract management).

You must understand the financial risks, no matter how small a project. For example, if you plan to do a job in one week (five workdays) and it extends to six days, then your profit is probably gone.

Selecting Qualified Management

The first step in planning is selecting qualified and adequate supervisors (management). Many failing jobs suffer from supervisors who are not fully qualified to perform the assigned duties on a particular job. You cannot afford to gamble on unqualified, inexperienced personnel. This business is tough enough for those who are qualified and experienced. When you select competent people to run a job, you are starting to minimize the risks. When you use people who are only marginally qualified, you are gambling. *(See Chapter 2 for more on selecting personnel.)*

You must also employ *enough* people. Some contractors tend to "go cheap" by shortchanging on supervisors, but think nothing of adding several carpenters when the job gets into trouble with the schedule. It may well have gotten into trouble because of inadequate project pre-planning. Studies of projects show that adequate and competent supervisors are one of the most important factors in successful projects.

Information Transfer

The second step is communication—or transfer of information to those who need it. Lack of communication is one of the biggest problems in the construction industry. In survey after survey, contractors, management, and field personnel rank lack of communication as the number one problem and risk.

Because the estimate is the first step in pre-planning, the information it generates must be well organized and transferred to whoever is managing the project. The estimate file is the basis for performing the work profitably and productively. *(See Chapter 8 for more on estimating.)* You must also update personnel about issues such as the preliminary schedule, pending changes, and billing procedures. Use

Checklist 21 to quickly bring supervisors up to speed.

Once the information has been properly transferred, the pre-planning process begins in earnest.

Familiarizing Personnel with the Contract

You are responsible for contract compliance for all of the work performed, whether it is performed by your own forces or by subcontractors. You must familiarize your employees and subs with the plans, specifications, and scope of work so that everyone involved with the project understands what is to be done. If this simple advice is followed, many punch list items will disappear, quality will be improved, and disputes can be avoided.

Planning the Project

The next steps involve developing an overall project plan. Planning isn't just a mental exercise. The plan must be action-oriented and realistic, and must be carried out. The secret of project management is to get others to *buy into the plan*—to have commitment and accountability for making the plan a reality. Planning should incorporate the thinking of all the parties who will be involved in the work, and must have everyone's commitment.

To many, control means monitoring the difference between planned and actual performance, and taking corrective action. *Real* control is working to prevent that difference and improve the plan so that corrective (and costly) action does not have to be taken. The checklists in this chapter can help you have real control.

Project Start-up

Just like the 747 pilot who reviews the takeoff checklist for every flight, you must also have a checklist to make sure nothing has been overlooked. Construction projects are not forgiving of glitches, which always cost someone time and money. Use Checklist 22 to review project start-up. The purpose of the Project Start-up Checklist is to make sure that the steps in the flow of construction are fully addressed up-front. The checklist should be tailored to each project, since there are big differences between building a new home, an addition, and doing a remodeling job.

Information Transfer

Use this checklist to gather the information that you will need to transfer to personnel. Check off each item when it is complete, and record the initials of the person who prepared it and the date.

	Prepared by:	Date:
☐ Subcontractor list.	_____	_____
☐ Vendor list.	_____	_____
☐ Key personnel list.	_____	_____
☐ Correspondence/telephone or e-mail memos.	_____	_____
☐ List of all unwritten promises made to owner (sales pitch).	_____	_____
☐ Contract with owner.	_____	_____
☐ Subcontracts.	_____	_____
☐ Extra copies of contract documents.	_____	_____
☐ Quantity survey/estimate.	_____	_____
☐ Definition of the type of costs included in the cost codes.	_____	_____
☐ List of special job-purchase items.	_____	
☐ Preliminary construction schedule.	_____	_____
☐ Description of pending changes.	_____	_____
☐ Building permit status.	_____	_____
☐ Billing procedures (including project's tax status or special tax procedures, payment for stored materials, and discounts).	_____	_____
☐ Extra work charges, including unit prices, overhead, and fees.	_____	_____

Checklist 21

Project Start-Up

Use this checklist to make sure that the steps in the flow of construction are fully addressed. The checklist should be tailored to each project. Record the initials of the person responsible for each task and the date the task is completed.

	Initials:	Date:

Transfer Phase

☐ Read contract documents carefully.

☐ Transfer documents to necessary parties.

☐ Identify major risks.

☐ Issue notice to proceed.

Pre-planning and Mobilization Phase

☐ Prepare schedule and begin pre-planning.

☐ Prepare a material handling plan.

☐ Establish safety and quality plans.

☐ Obtain permits.

☐ Provide builder's risk and other required insurance.

☐ Define crew responsibilities.

☐ Establish priorities.

☐ Post required legal notices (OSHA, etc.).

☐ Designate which set of drawings and specifications are to be kept on job site.

Notes:

_____

_____

_____

Checklist 22

92

Project Start-Up *(continued)*

Job Site Administrative Phase

☐ Establish an office filing system. _____ _____

☐ Finalize all subcontracts. _____ _____

☐ Schedule periodic review meetings with owner
(and architect). _____ _____

☐ Schedule inspections with building officials. _____ _____

☐ Complete a submittal log. _____ _____

☐ Commit to all major purchases. _____ _____

☐ Review labor agreements, if any. _____ _____

☐ Set up a change order log. _____ _____

☐ Get written authorization for changes. _____ _____

☐ Set up a daily log. _____ _____

☐ Plan each week's activities. _____ _____

☐ Coordinate subcontractors. _____ _____

☐ Manage material and equipment deliveries. _____ _____

Notes:

_____

_____

_____

_____

_____

_____

Checklist 22

Cost Accounting

It's important to have an effective cost accounting system that everyone in the company uses and understands. For example, small contractors often fail to recognize the need to accurately represent and account for their time on the job. This means reporting non-productive time separately from productive time. (For example, we might say we worked eight hours, when in fact we spent two of those hours waiting for material or for the area to warm up.) An efficient cost accounting system is an essential management tool. Cost reporting systems that are outdated, inaccurate, or difficult to use should be thrown out. Field personnel must have timely data to know what they are to do and have enough time to take corrective action. They lose out by mis-reporting or failing to report cost information, and destroy any opportunity you may have to take corrective action. Inaccurately reported cost information may also be worthless in a claim or litigation situation.

Material Handling Plan

The way materials are handled has a big effect on the job cost. Formulating a plan for handling materials is a key aspect of planning the job. The right materials and equipment must be delivered to the job site at the right time, handled properly (so that there is no damage due to poor storage), and installed, tested, and checked properly. If one of these "rights" becomes a "wrong," installation time is increased, and so is the cost. Material management involves risks at every step of the way. Illustration 5.4 is a log that can help you keep track of materials by recording important information, such as quantity ordered and received, delivery dates, and so forth.

Project Control and Record Keeping

When the project begins, your pre-planning is put to the test, and you will have to make adjustments as needed. You must verify that planned events have occurred (or will occur) to protect yourself against losing control of the job. You must also record important events on the construction project. Documentation is as essential as pre-planning to the success of a project.

Logs are a key element in project control. Your daily log should be used to note the weather, significant events, and progress at the end of each day. Even the smallest jobs should have a daily log. If you are working on multiple small projects, you need to also keep track of your management time. A regular method of tracking details is also necessary for good project control.

Illustrations 5.2-5.5 are types of logs that should be used on each project. They include logs to keep track of change orders, requests for information, material status, and submittals.

Change Order Log

Project _____   Job No. _____

Request for Proposal				Proposal							Authorization		
				To Subs (list)	From Subs (list)	To Owner		Days Elapsed	Approval		Notice to Proceed	Change Order No.	
No.	Date	Description	RFI No.			Date	$ Amount		Date	$ Amount			

Illustration 5.2

95

Request For Information (RFI) Log

Project _____ Architect _____ Owner _____

Request Number	Date of Request	Description	Plan Page No. (if applicable)	Disposition	Disposition Date	Days Elapsed	Effect*

*Record Effect on Occurrence Report

Illustration 5.3

Material Status Report Log

Project _____ Job No. _____

Material Item	Number (if applicable)	Delivery Date		Quantity		Submittal Date		Approval Date	
		Promised	Actual	Ordered	Received	Expected	Actual	Expected	Actual

Illustration 5.4

Submittal Log

Project _____ Job No. _____

Item Description	Manufacturer Product Number	Drawing/Sample	Submittal Dates		Approval Status*	Given to Sub
			To Us	To Owner		

*A = approved; AAN = approved as noted; R = rejected; RR = revise & resubmit
NOTE: Alternating lines are dashed to allow for resubmittals of the same item.

Illustration 5.5

Managing Changes to the Plan

Changes are inevitable, despite the best-laid plans and promises. Wise builders accept this fact and plan accordingly, but do not make changes or spend money without proper authority and documentation. If you proceed with changes without clear direction, you risk not being paid or having to do the work over. Clear and undisputed directions should come before you make any changes on a project.

Changes are a problem in the construction industry because they can create confusion and delays. Prompt and well-documented communication is the key to solving this problem. You must start with a clear understanding of the change. Then you must communicate your understanding to all parties who will be affected by it.

All job site supervisors should be responsible for changes and for communicating the associated requirements. They should also be responsible for identifying changed conditions. This means they must recognize items that represent extra costs, and those for which the owner should pay. You should also not get into the habit of giving away "freebies" to customers. Your crew may get involved with work on the job that they think is nice to do, but is an entirely different project than the one they are there for. If the job is to install a new window, the customer should not expect you to repair hidden damaged areas at no extra cost. Illustration 5.6 shows the difference between changes that occur because conditions differ from those described in the contract documents and changes that are time-related. Compensable and noncompensable delays are also shown.

Checklist 23 will help you develop a strategy to manage changes and a system for controlling change procedures. Documenting your communications to all parties affected by the change is the key to managing changes correctly.

Differing site conditions (such as discovering boulders while excavating for a basement when they were not indicated in the soils report) is a special case of changes that occur frequently and can have dramatic effects on the project. Checklist 24 is a separate Differing Site Conditions Checklist.

99

Job Filing System

The job site filing system is essential not only for the duration of the job, but often years later (if there are claims, litigation, etc.). Checklist 25 shows a sample of a filing system that has proven to be extremely effective, providing an easy way to find information when you need it. A description of the job filing system should be distributed to all who will be using it to make sure you end up with consistent reports and reviews.

Early Indicator System

Finally, you need to make sure that your plan is working as intended. There must be an effective method in place for gathering information about the progress of your project. It is not enough to simply perform a walk-through and ask crews why the concrete placement is overrunning the budget. If you learn about problems early on, you will have enough time to take aggressive action to stop the overruns.

Identifying Changes and Delays

Changes	
Contract Documents	**Time-Related**
Defective design	Acceleration
Discrepancy in plans	Constructive acceleration
Added, altered, or deleted work	Suspension of work
Differing site conditions	Out-of-sequence work
	Overtime
	Stand-by

Delays	
Compensable	**Non-Compensable**
Owner's act or neglect	Adverse weather conditions
A/E's act or neglect	(unless contract indicates otherwise)
Other prime's act or neglect	Casualties beyond control (e.g.,
Changes to work	vandalism, accidents, fires, floods, riots
Owner-authorized delay	Acts of God

Illustration 5.6

100

Managing Changes

Use this checklist to help you manage changes efficiently.

- ☐ Identify source of change:

    - ☐ Field directives.

    - ☐ Marked-up drawings.

    - ☐ Correspondence.

    - ☐ Formal change request.

    - ☐ Differing site conditions.

    - ☐ Suspension of work.

    - ☐ Overtime or stand-by.

- ☐ Ensure notification of change:

    - ☐ Written directive from owner.

    - ☐ Written notice to owner.
      (Reserve your rights.)

    - ☐ Written directive to subs.

    - ☐ Written directive to field personnel.

- ☐ Document and control change:

    - ☐ Keep changes log.

    - ☐ Separate cost codes.

- ☐ Price all items.

- ☐ Separate direct and indirect costs.

- ☐ Enforce timely receipt of subcontractor and vendor quotes.

- ☐ Identify changes in other logs (e.g., comments in RFI log).

- ☐ Update schedule to see effects.

- ☐ Initiate changes:

    - ☐ Make sure crews know exactly what to do.

    - ☐ Execute subcontractor and vendor change orders as soon as possible.

    - ☐ Include changes on pay applications as soon as possible.

    - ☐ Integrate changes into cost accounting as soon as possible.

    - ☐ Review change log weekly.

    - ☐ Do not let outstanding changes pile up.

    - ☐ Update as-built drawings.

Notes:

_____

_____

Checklist 23

Differing Site Conditions

Most differing site conditions occur within the first 25% of the job, and a change in sequence or a delay can greatly impact your project's success. Use this checklist to manage differing site conditions.

☐ Read the differing site conditions clause in the contract.

☐ Give immediate, written notification to owner and ask for direction.

☐ Document what the actual conditions are versus what conditions were indicated by the contract documents. (If conditions are unusual and differ from those ordinarily encountered, show that you could not have reasonably anticipated them. Show that the pre-bid site investigation was adequate.)

☐ Take pictures.

☐ Get owner's representative to examine the site immediately.

☐ If in doubt, bring an expert consultant to the site immediately.

☐ Develop a price for additional time, materials, and equipment required.

☐ Get written directive from owner to proceed with the work.

☐ Set up separate cost codes and track direct and indirect costs associated with the extra work.

☐ Make sure daily logs record extra work done each day, including crew, equipment, and time specifics.

☐ Update the schedule to determine what additional activities are affected.

☐ If the change interferes with your meeting the original schedule (and you are still required to meet the end date), document the extra cost (e.g., extra crew) associated with accelerating any part of the work.

Notes:

_____

_____

_____

_____

_____

Checklist 24

Filing System for Job Site Documents

Use this checklist to make sure you address all documents that should be organized and filed as you plan the project.

- ☐ Pre-construction documents:
    - ☐ Architect's estimate.
    - ☐ Engineering studies.
    - ☐ Soils information.
    - ☐ Utilities information.
    - ☐ Preliminary schedules.
    - ☐ Other
- ☐ Bid documents:
    - ☐ Plans.
    - ☐ Specifications.
    - ☐ Contract documents.
    - ☐ General terms and conditions.
    - ☐ Special terms and conditions.
    - ☐ Pre-bid meetings.
    - ☐ Bids, abstract of bids.
    - ☐ Bid verification.
    - ☐ Bid schedules, subcontractor quotes.
    - ☐ Quantity takeoffs.
- ☐ Estimate.
- ☐ Subcontractors' estimates.
- ☐ Site inspection notes.
- ☐ Contract Documents:
    - ☐ Letter of intent.
    - ☐ Contract with owner.
    - ☐ Contract with subcontractors.
    - ☐ Notice to proceed.
    - ☐ Change orders and logs, listed by date.
    - ☐ Extra work order.
    - ☐ Proposals and log, listed by date.
    - ☐ Request for Proposals (RFP), listed by date.
- ☐ Project schedules and documentation:
    - ☐ Contract schedule and updates.
    - ☐ Shop drawing and submittal logs.
- ☐ Claims and backcharges:
    - ☐ Contractor.
    - ☐ Subcontractor.
    - ☐ Owner.
    - ☐ A/E.

Checklist 25

Filing System for Job Site Documents *(continued)*

- ☐ Meeting minutes/daily reports:
  - ☐ Owner.
  - ☐ Architect.
  - ☐ Pre-construction conference.
  - ☐ Project management meetings.
  - ☐ Negotiations.
  - ☐ Daily logs and reports.
- ☐ Correspondence:
  - ☐ To owner.
  - ☐ From owner.
  - ☐ To subcontractor.
  - ☐ From subcontractor.
  - ☐ To suppliers.
  - ☐ From suppliers.
  - ☐ To architect.
  - ☐ From architect.
  - ☐ Sketches or details provided by the architect.

- ☐ Construction changes directives.
- ☐ Other
  - ☐ Transmittals.
  - ☐ Request for Information: log, file.
  - ☐ Occurrence Reports: log, file.
- ☐ Job cost reports
  - ☐ Reports (usually monthly; include all costs).
  - ☐ Labor (usually weekly, include only labor accounts, but in greater detail).
  - ☐ Material (usually monthly).
  - ☐ Equipment (usually weekly).
- ☐ Photos.
- ☐ Warranties.
- ☐ Legal files.
- ☐ Miscellaneous.

Notes:

_____

_____

_____

Checklist 25

104

The Early Indicator Checklist (Checklist 26) is an important control tool for all jobs. It turns early warning signals into early management actions.

The project team must provide the necessary early warning signals, so that action can be taken while it can still do some good. If information comes too late, it merely confirms that something bad has happened, when nothing can be done about it.

Planning and Scheduling Software

There are a number of excellent and inexpensive planning and project management tools. Among them are Microsoft Project. Illustration 5.7 and 5.8 are examples of a Microsoft Project application showing the schedule for the construction of a new house and a bathroom remodel. It is an excellent monitoring tool for seeing where you are at any given time. This system can also include other activities (submittals, deliveries, inspections, and so forth). It is a simple way of planning, but, more important, it is a tool for getting the team to work together toward the project's goals and schedule. *(Note: Before you buy software, make sure you understand your needs and acquire a system that is right for your company. See Chapter 2 for more on implementing computer software in your business.)*

What We Have Learned

Effective project planning is key to success. Once you have created a thorough and realistic plan of what needs to be done, the duration and sequence of each activity can be accurately scheduled. The basic project steps that need to be thoroughly planned for are listed in Checklist 27. If there is one principle that cannot be overemphasized, it is that planning is a management function—a proactive, forecasting, and control function.

A final word of advice: most contractors know how to start a job, but only successful ones know how to finish. As the job progresses, the urgency tends to diminish. The successful builder understands that when things are going well, you need to keep the momentum.

Early Indicator Project Status Checklist

Use this checklist to help determine and take action on potential problems. Review and update it on a regular basis throughout the life of the project.

	Yes	No	Date
Estimate/Budget			
☐ Has the construction budget been developed/balanced?	☐	☐	_____
☐ Have change orders been integrated into the construction budget?	☐	☐	_____
☐ Have any significant estimate problems been identified?	☐	☐	_____

Comments: _____

_____

Change Order Status			
☐ Are we getting a written directive from the owner before proceeding with a change?	☐	☐	_____
☐ Are changes being processed in a timely manner?	☐	☐	_____
☐ Are there disputes regarding scope pricing?	☐	☐	_____
☐ Do subs have claims for change orders that are in dispute?	☐	☐	_____
☐ Is the owner reasonable in responding to changes in a timely manner?	☐	☐	_____
☐ Do change orders require a lender's approval?	☐	☐	_____

Comments: _____

_____

Clarifications			
☐ Do we maintain an RFI log to track problems and/or questions that arise?	☐	☐	_____
☐ Does the owner (or architect) take action and/or respond in a timely manner to resolve issues?	☐	☐	_____

Checklist 26

Early Indicator Project Status Checklist *(continued)*

	Yes	No	Date
☐ Are there outstanding RFIs or problems affecting the work?	☐	☐	_____

Comments: _____

_____

Schedule

	Yes	No	Date
☐ Is the schedule regularly updated?	☐	☐	_____
☐ Does the updated schedule incorporate change/delay effects?	☐	☐	_____
☐ Is the project on schedule in accordance with the updated schedule?	☐	☐	_____
☐ Do we have adequate personnel and equipment to maintain the schedule?	☐	☐	_____
☐ Are there any problems with anticipated late deliveries of critical materials?	☐	☐	_____
☐ Will there be material delivery problems resulting from the impact of changes (change orders, proposals, etc.)?	☐	☐	_____
☐ Has the owner been advised of any delays affecting anticipated turnover dates?	☐	☐	_____
☐ Is the project experiencing delays/interference from the owner (or his agents)?	☐	☐	_____
☐ If so, have we given timely notification in accordance with contract requirements?	☐	☐	_____

Comments: _____

_____

Checklist 26

Early Indicator Project Status Checklist (continued)

	Yes	No	Date

Costs

☐ Does the cost report indicate any significant variances in major work accounts? ☐ ☐ _____

   ☐ If so, what is the approximate cost incurred to date? ☐ ☐ _____

Comments: _____

_____

Billings

☐ Are billings current? ☐ ☐ _____

☐ Does this project show costs in excess of billings? ☐ ☐ _____

☐ Do we bill for work performed on unapproved changes? ☐ ☐ _____

☐ Are progress billings generally approved as submitted (e.g., reasonable adjustments only)? ☐ ☐ _____

☐ Do we receive payments on time as per contract? ☐ ☐ _____

Comments: _____

_____

Subcontractors

☐ Do we have any problems with subcontractors? ☐ ☐ _____

☐ Do we have a good relationship with each of our subcontractors? ☐ ☐ _____

☐ Do we hold regular meetings? ☐ ☐ _____

☐ Are any subs unable or unwilling to provide adequate manpower to meet production schedule? ☐ ☐ _____

☐ Are any subs unable or unwilling to provide acceptable quality workmanship? ☐ ☐ _____

☐ Are any subs requesting assistance in material management or expediting? ☐ ☐ _____

Checklist 26

108

Early Indicator Project Status Checklist *(continued)*

	Yes	No	Date
☐ Are pay requests realistic in view of work performed?	☐	☐	_____
☐ Are we obtaining lien releases from all major suppliers to our subcontractors as per subcontract conditions?	☐	☐	_____
☐ Do we have current certificates of insurance on file for each subcontractor?	☐	☐	_____

Comments: _____

_____

Other

☐ How are the relationships between us and: Poor – Excellent (1-10)

☐ The owner? _____

☐ The architect? _____

	Yes	No	Date
☐ Are daily diaries being maintained?	☐	☐	_____
☐ Are all logs being maintained in accordance with company procedures?	☐	☐	_____
☐ Are we experiencing any unusual or unreasonable inspection requirements from the owner (or the architect) or inspectors?	☐	☐	_____
☐ Have we encountered any unexpected unusual conditions that may impact the project?	☐	☐	_____
☐ Have we deviated from the plans and/or specifications?	☐	☐	_____
☐ If so, have we received written approval from the owner and/or architect?	☐	☐	_____

Comments: _____

Checklist 26

109

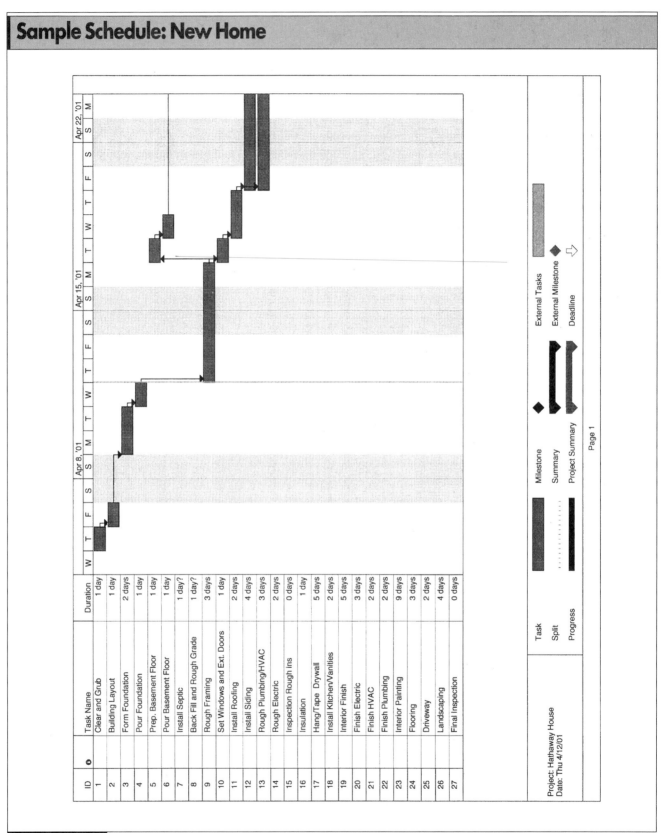

The Gantt chart includes the following tasks:

ID	●	Task Name	Duration
1		Clear and Grub	1 day
2		Building Layout	1 day
3		Form Foundation	2 days
4		Pour Foundation	1 day
5		Prep. Basement Floor	1 day
6		Pour Basement Floor	1 day
7		Install Septic	1 day?
8		Back Fill and Rough Grade	1 day?
9		Rough Framing	3 days
10		Set Windows and Ext. Doors	1 day
11		Install Roofing	2 days
12		Install Siding	4 days
13		Rough Plumbing/HVAC	3 days
14		Rough Electric	2 days
15		Inspection Rough Ins	0 days
16		Insulation	1 day
17		Hang/Tape Drywall	5 days
18		Install Kitchen/Vanities	2 days
19		Interior Finish	5 days
20		Finish Electric	3 days
21		Finish HVAC	2 days
22		Finish Plumbing	2 days
23		Interior Painting	9 days
24		Flooring	3 days
25		Driveway	2 days
26		Landscaping	4 days
27		Final Inspection	0 days

Project: Hathaway House
Date: Thu 4/12/01

Task
Split
Progress

Milestone
Summary
Project Summary

External Tasks
External Milestone
Deadline

Page 1

Illustration 5.7

110

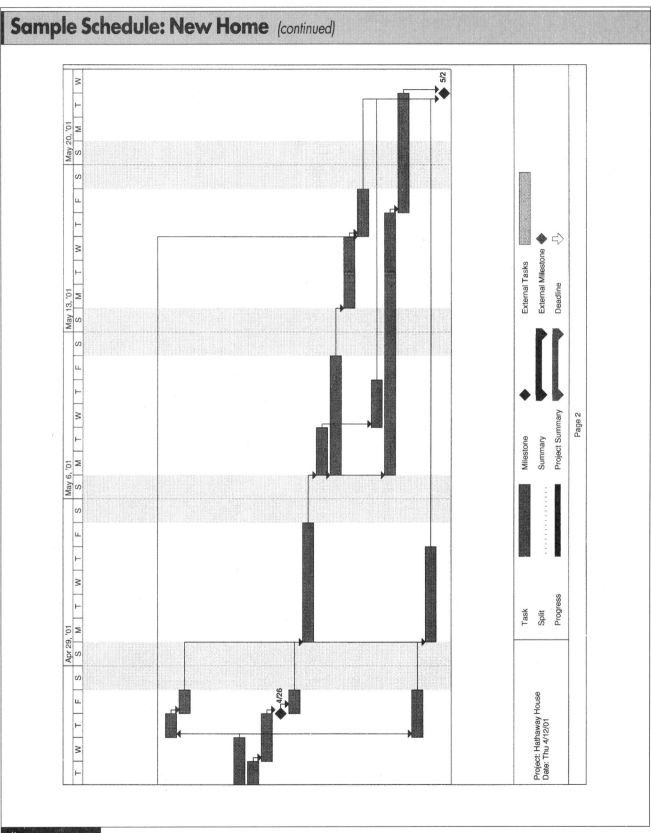

Milestone ◆   External Tasks

Task   Summary   External Milestone ◆

Split   Project Summary   Deadline ⇨

Progress

Project: Hathaway House
Date: Thu 4/12/01

Page 2

Illustration 5.7

Sample Schedule: Bathroom Remodel

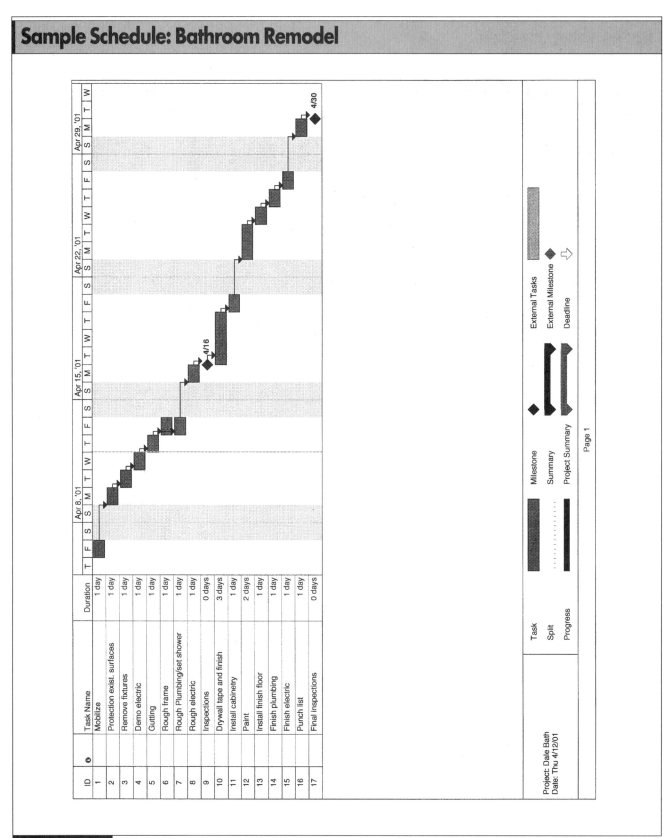

ID	❶	Task Name	Duration
1		Mobilize	1 day
2		Protection exist. surfaces	1 day
3		Remove fixtures	1 day
4		Demo electric	1 day
5		Gutting	1 day
6		Rough frame	1 day
7		Rough Plumbing/set shower	1 day
8		Rough electric	1 day
9		Inspections	0 days
10		Drywall tape and finish	3 days
11		Install cabinetry	1 day
12		Paint	2 days
13		Install finish floor	1 day
14		Finish plumbing	1 day
15		Finish electric	1 day
16		Punch list	1 day
17		Final inspections	0 days

Project: Dale Bath
Date: Thu 4/12/01

Task		Milestone	◆	External Tasks
Split		Summary	◆▬▬◆	External Milestone ◆
Progress		Project Summary	◆▬▬◆	Deadline ⇩

Page 1

Illustration 5.8

112

Project Steps to Plan

Use this checklist to make sure you address all issues that need planning throughout the project.

Getting Ready

- ☐ Submittals
- ☐ Site protection
- ☐ Notices posted
- ☐ Insurance/bond
- ☐ P.O.s
- ☐ Subcontracts
- ☐ Crew set-up
- ☐ Utility connections
- ☐ Mobilization
- ☐ Job schedule
- ☐ Permits

Coming to Grade

- ☐ Inspections
- ☐ Capping off lines (utilities, water, sewer, etc.)
- ☐ Demolition
- ☐ Footings
- ☐ Dampproofing
- ☐ Termite protection
- ☐ Excavation
- ☐ Site work

- ☐ Site protection
- ☐ Two-week (look-ahead) plan

Weather-Tight (Dry-In)

- ☐ Inspections
- ☐ Exterior doors
- ☐ Windows in exterior walls
- ☐ Roof framed, sheathed
- ☐ Framing
- ☐ Subs notified
- ☐ Crew organized
- ☐ Material storage protection
- ☐ Water filtration
- ☐ Acclimation of materials to interior humidity
- ☐ Quality plan
- ☐ Two-week (look-ahead) plan

Rough-Ins

- ☐ Inspections
- ☐ Mechanical
- ☐ Plumbing
- ☐ Electrical
- ☐ Walls and ceilings

Checklist 27

113

Project Steps to Plan *(continued)*

☐ Two-week (look-ahead) plan

Finishes

☐ Interior trim

☐ Paint

☐ Walls and ceiling

☐ Siding

☐ Inspections

☐ Cleanup

☐ Landscaping

☐ Carpet

☐ Cabinetry

☐ Fixtures

☐ "SMART" installations (computerized systems, such as lighting, burglar)

☐ Complete drywall

☐ Two-week (look-ahead) plan

Close-Out

☐ Lien releases

☐ Final change order negotiations

☐ Warranties

☐ As-builts complete

☐ Appliance and other material, product care information and warranties delivered to customer

☐ Final inspection and permit signoff

☐ Close-out documents (such as deed registration)

☐ Occupancy permit

☐ Owner training

Notes:

_____

_____

_____

_____

_____

_____

Checklist 27

Quality Control and Inspection

Our Company:

- ☑ Has a solid reputation for quality.
- ☑ Makes sure all personnel are trained properly.
- ☑ Knows contract requirements and enforces them.
- ☑ Knows building codes and standards and enforces them.
- ☑ Has very few punch list items on projects.
- ☑ Continually improves techniques and stays up-to-date with new methods.

Chapter Six

Quality Control and Inspection

Today quality is not just something to aim for; it is an essential ingredient in any kind of long-term success. Customers demand it, and many builders and remodelers focus their entire marketing strategy on their reputation for quality workmanship. More and more builders are discovering that "doing it right the first time" is an important way to guarantee profit and improve cash flow. These builders are committed to quality as a practice, rather than an ideal. They build in quality, rather than wait until the work has been finished and then look for mistakes to be corrected. Quality should be a race without a finish line, with the entire organization constantly striving to raise the bar of performance.

Quality is made up of many components that are linked together to create a sound final product. These essential elements include:

- Closely monitoring and documenting project expectations, procedures, and the final result.

- Following building codes, regulations, safety and quality standards, and manufacturers' guidelines.

- Meeting warranty requirements.

- Using experienced craftspeople and monitoring their work.

- Using appropriate materials, equipment, tools, and construction procedures.

- Providing customer satisfaction.

In many ways, quality workmanship depends on a quality company as its foundation—one that has a clear plan for future growth, for development of employees, and for commitment to do the best job possible. In this sense, a quality project depends on successful management of *all* aspects of the company, and is closely linked to all other chapters of this book. Contractors can lose work not only because of poor workmanship, but because of the attitude or behavior of workers or a failure to adequately clean up after a job is done. Quality must resonate throughout every function of the company; it must be inherent in every activity, every attitude, and every relationship.

The first step in your company's "quality culture" is to establish a policy that requires quality as its core value, and to make sure that all employees buy into it and live up to it. Your policy could state, "Our company is committed to perform every function to ensure customer satisfaction while making a profit."

Someone once said that freedom is like bread—you go on earning it every day. The same can be said of quality. It is easy to let it slip away unless it is given constant attention. For this reason, it is recommended that you give every customer an evaluation form to rate your work, no matter how small the project. *(See Checklist 31.)*

Professional Standards of Quality

Some definitions of quality can be found in the recommendations of institutes that represent building product manufacturers, such as the Window and Door Manufacturers Association (WDMA), the Tile Council of America (TCA), and the Engineered Wood Association (APA). Their guidelines are distributed through publications and electronic products, on the Internet, and in training sessions and videos. These recommendations are based on field and laboratory research. If there is a conflict between an industry standard and an explicit contract requirement, the contract usually prevails. Manufacturers provide their own installation guidelines for particular products. Compliance with these instructions is often linked to product warranties. *(See the "Resources" section for manufacturer contact information.)*

Quality standards are also set forth by professional associations, such as the National Association of Home Builders, the National Roofing Contractors Association, and the Painting and Decorating Contractors of America, all of which represent contractors in the industry. These organizations also provide training (in various media and in local and national conferences) on current and correct construction methods. *(See the "Resources" section for contact information).*

Many states require licensing to verify that you are capable of meeting the standards of quality work. Depending on where you work, you may need to get a builder's or specialty license. Many builders establish a quality reputation with credentials such as certification as a Graduate Remodeler (offered by NAHB), for example.

Meeting Codes and Standards

As a builder or remodeler, you may also be the designer, engineer, and specialty craftsman responsible for a construction project. In this case, you must be responsible for complying with codes and standards, which are designed to protect life and property. Up to four different levels of building codes (federal, state, local, and model or the *International Building Code®* or *International Residential Code®*) may apply to a project, and are normally identified within the local building code or by the local zoning board. In designing and building a project, you may need to consult local building code requirements and discuss them with members of the building department (sometimes along with the architect and owner). Interpretations of codes may vary between your local building department offices or even between officials in the same office. Be sure to find out in advance what these interpretations are—not after the fact when you have to tear out work that an inspector rejected. Also remember, unless you are licensed, beware of doing extensive design work (especially structural) without the review of a licensed PE.

Developing a good working relationship with local building departments is critical for a successful contractor. The relationship should be professional and built on honesty. If you are not confident in your ability to build to code, or are reluctant to do so, then you may be in the wrong business.

You should understand the codes and standards requirements for each project, and should compile them and make them available to all supervisors on the site. When questions come up, don't guess about how to interpret the code. Instead consult local officials and professional associations. Building codes and standards you should be familiar with include the following.

- **The American Concrete Institute (ACI)** develops standards for design and construction that involves concrete and related materials. ACI 318 is referenced by the *International Building Code®* and all model codes, including the *Uniform Building Code™*, the *BOCA® National Building Code*, and the *Standard Building Code©*.

119

- **The Americans with Disabilities Act (ADA)** is a federal civil rights law enacted in 1990 that requires building accessibility for people with disabilities. It applies to new construction for buildings with public accommodations or commercial use. Several states have adopted the ADA Act Guidelines (ADAAG) as a code requirement (with some amendments).

- **The American National Standards Institute (ANSI)** regulates the nation's standardization for products and work. Many local and state governments and other agencies have adopted ANSI's voluntary standards.

- **The American Society for Testing and Materials (ASTM)** develops standards based on test methods for materials, products, and practices for building products including metals, paints, and plastics, as well as consumer products and electronics. More than 10,000 ASTM standards are published annually, and many are referenced in building codes and regulations.

- *The International Building Code®* (IBC), and *International Residential Code®* (IRC), first published in the year 2000, represent unified national codes that cover construction, fire protection, egress, accessibility, mechanical, plumbing, and other topics. The International Code Council® (ICC), which governs the IBC and IRC, was founded in 1994 by the three major model code organizations—Building Officials and Code Administrators International (BOCA), the International Conference of Building Officials (ICBO), and the Southern Building Code Congress International (SBCCI).

- **National Fire Protection Association International (NFPA)** provides fire, electrical, and life safety codes and standards and maintains the *National Electrical Code® (NFPA 70)* and the *Life Safety Code® (NFPA 101®)*, among many others. The *Life Safety Code®* sets the minimum design requirements for protection from fire and other emergencies. Many states mandate compliance with this code.

- **Underwriters Laboratories (UL)** is a product safety testing and certification organization that tests and lists construction systems and components for qualities such as fire- and wind-resistance and has listings for electrical equipment and products.

The contact information for these organizations—including addresses, phone numbers, and Web sites—can be found in the "Resources" section at the back of this book.

A final note about meeting codes: there is no need to "overbuild" in order to comply with codes. Using oversized stock (unless designed into the project to meet a customer's particular needs or desires) is not necessary and may cause you to be less competitive.

Quality in Design

The first step toward a quality finished project is putting together a thorough scope of work and design that meets building codes and standards and is based on sound engineering principles. The design should also meet both the customer's requirements and your own standards. Some customers may require that the quality exceed the minimum requirements set forth by codes and standards. A quality design also includes addressing the following issues:

- Making sure whoever designs the project has the necessary expertise to do so. (Sometimes small contractors are required to have a registered architect or PE submit their plans for approval by building officials.)
- Making sure whoever designs the project is familiar with site conditions and any special considerations.
- Making sure the contract documents are clear, complete, and accurate. *(See Chapter 4 for more on contracts.)*

The quality of a project is described in the design phase. Meeting the design standard set by the contract documents is often the best measure of quality. Communication is also key to a quality design. Without it, some design elements may not be clear, and conflicts can easily arise.

Quality in Construction

Project quality also depends on competent personnel and proper construction procedures and materials. Even the best plan for quality assurance will crumble under incapable workmanship or inappropriate materials. *(See Chapters 2, 3, and 7 for selecting and managing capable personnel, including subcontractors and other employees.)* Two approaches to proper business management that are commonly used in construction are *quality assurance* and *quality control*.

Quality Assurance

Quality assurance (QA) involves putting together a plan and using standards, policies, and procedures to make sure the project runs as smoothly as possible. QA makes sure that:

- You have a plan in place that sets forth the standards of acceptance and is communicated to all who will perform and accept work.
- You document in writing all rights and responsibilities.
- You provide comprehensive submittals about types and quality of equipment and materials.
- You use materials that match the design standards described in the contract.
- You use proper testing and inspection methods.
- You reject deficient and non-conforming work—and correct it immediately.
- You follow all manufacturers' recommendations.

As the contractor, you are always responsible for doing a quality job whether there is a contract or not. Whether you are remodeling a bathroom or building a home, your goal is to ensure that the job is done right, according to the agreement the parties have made.

Put your expectations for the project—in terms of standards of workmanship, policies, and procedures—in writing. That way, you can easily judge the quality of your project by comparing the actual outcome to your original plan and intentions.

Quality Control

Quality control (QC) is where "the rubber meets the road." It isn't *planning* quality anymore; it is *doing* quality work and checking to make sure it is done correctly. QC consists of the specific steps you take to carry out your quality assurance (QA) plan. QC includes things like regular inspections of the work, making sure subcontractors are certified installers of materials and products, and getting feedback from customers about how well you did.

Meetings and inspections are particularly important to ensure quality control. They provide the opportunity to bring up and address problems before they become serious.

As with QA, QC requires keeping records, especially of construction steps and procedures. If you keep a record of what you do, how you do it, and when, you will create an accurate and reliable log that can be easily referenced if problems arise.

Checklist 28 can be used to check the quality of your company and its overall performance. Checklist 29 can be used for project QA and QC—from start to finish.

Project Drawings and On-the-Job Sketches

One of the best ways to ensure quality in construction is by creating accurate sets of drawings along the way. Some contractors provide design and construction services. Others work from architects' designs. Even if an architect designed the project, homeowners may still rely on you to sketch details showing how one element will relate to another. You might also need to submit sketches to building officials or show your crew a construction method.

As a builder or remodeler, you should be able to visualize details, and put them on paper in the form of a sketch. If you can illustrate in a drawing what you intend to build, everyone will have a better understanding of what they should expect.

Accurate drawings—whether quick sketches on the spot or more time-consuming, detailed drawings—are an ingredient in a quality job. They keep everyone on track and minimize surprises.

A few tips:

- **Draw to scale.** Sketches not drawn to scale are misleading, both to crews and customers. Your drawings don't have to be works of art or complex, but need to be accurate.

- **Include all elements and steps,** even though you may think they are obvious. Leaving something out can mislead customers and confuse workers.

- **Don't overdraw.** Show the parts of the project *exactly* as they will be. Don't take liberties to make things look more elaborate than what is planned.

Quality Program

Use this checklist to check the quality of your company and its overall performance. Do you:

☐ Stand by company values: quality and pride throughout the company?

☐ Hire only licensed, qualified, and competent field tradespeople and subcontractors?

☐ Return all calls promptly?

☐ Read the agreement carefully?

☐ Plan the job properly, focusing on quality workmanship?

☐ Inform crews and subs of your quality standards, and show them how to do things right?

☐ Inspect materials carefully when they arrive on site?

☐ Return and replace defective materials?

☐ Properly plan and check critical activities, including the following?
(Some items on the list will vary by project.)

  ☐ Grades
  ☐ Dimensions
  ☐ Flashing (windows, roof, chimney and other penetrations, masonry)
  ☐ Concrete finishes
  ☐ Plumb and level of horizontal and vertical members
  ☐ Every step in roof construction
  ☐ Proper interior finishes
  ☐ All code requirements

☐ Make sure the building inspector is properly scheduled (especially for items such as inspections of overhead and concealed areas)?

☐ Reject poor workmanship? Do you stop and address it before the problem escalates?

Checklist 28

Planning and Managing Quality

Use this checklist to help you develop and manage a plan for quality.

Quality Plan

☐ Review the scope of work and plans for quality requirements.

☐ Review industry standards and manufacturers' warranty requirements.

☐ Review applicable building codes and standards.

☐ Go over the above information with personnel and subcontractors.

Managing Quality

☐ Present quality standards to crew members.

☐ Establish "finish standards" for such trades as drywall/plaster, painting, and masonry.

☐ Check on new work activities as they are beginning to see if it they are being done right early on, rather than waiting until the work is under way or complete.

☐ Schedule inspections to occur on a timely basis.

☐ File documentation (such as test results) in a safe place, organized for easy access.

☐ Hold a "lessons learned" session after the project is complete to see how the company can improve.

Notes:

_____

_____

_____

_____

_____

_____

_____

Checklist 29

- **Don't assume that everyone understands your drawings.** Explain to customers and crews what your drawings show, and be sure they thoroughly understand this information.

- **If you can't draw accurately, find someone who can.** You might have someone with CAD experience do some quick sketches for you.

Accurate drawings help ensure the job is done right—and that everyone is on the same track.

Illustrations 6.1 and 6.2 are examples of drawings you might create for remodeling or new construction projects—as part of the official design drawings—or as a tool for working with your crew.

Training

Quality craftsmanship requires qualified, experienced, and trained workers. To continue to raise the bar of quality for your company, training should be an ongoing effort, and not a one-time or one-session event. You will improve the quality of all your projects if you encourage subs and other workers to advance their skills through professional education, such as offered by technical schools, community colleges, and professional associations. You can also improve your own performance by taking these kinds of courses.

You play a major role in training crews by simply showing them how some things should be done on each project, rather than assuming they instinctually know. At the very least, you should have seasoned professionals work with apprentices to provide on-site training. New personnel should be trained in quality control and company policies, as well as in safety procedures and technical skills. Even a tradesman with years of technical experience can jeopardize quality if he performs a task differently from what you intended. Sketching the work to be done and discussing procedures are part of job site training.

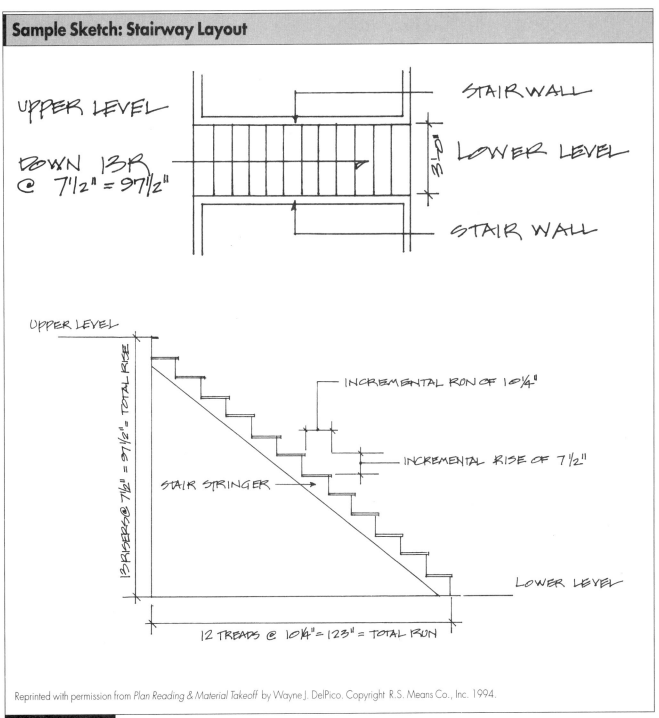

UPPER LEVEL

DOWN 13R
@ 7½" = 97½"

STAIR WALL

LOWER LEVEL

3'-0"

STAIR WALL

UPPER LEVEL

13 RISERS @ 7½" = 97½" = TOTAL RISE

INCREMENTAL RUN OF 10¼"

INCREMENTAL RISE OF 7½"

STAIR STRINGER

LOWER LEVEL

12 TREADS @ 10¼" = 123" = TOTAL RUN

Reprinted with permission from *Plan Reading & Material Takeoff* by Wayne J. DelPico. Copyright R.S. Means Co., Inc. 1994.

Illustration 6.1

Employee Performance Reviews

Evaluate worker performance on a regular basis—and document your observations. Ask employees to evaluate their own performance as well, taking note of strengths and weaknesses and areas needing improvement. After these evaluations have been conducted a few times, you can compare them to make sure employees are making progress as planned.

Sample Sketch: Roof Layout

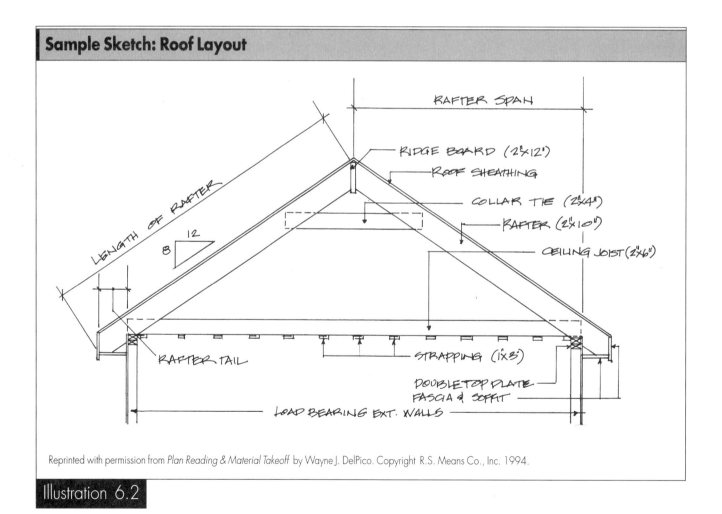

Reprinted with permission from *Plan Reading & Material Takeoff* by Wayne J. DelPico. Copyright R.S. Means Co., Inc. 1994.

Illustration 6.2

Quality Materials, Tools, and Equipment

Achieving quality in construction also depends on the quality of the tools, equipment, and materials provided. Even the most skilled craftsman would find it difficult to produce top workmanship using poor quality materials or inappropriate tools. Make sure all workers use tools and equipment that consistently perform reliably and safely, and materials that meet design specifications and/or code and standards requirements.

Avoiding Workmanship Problems

When workmanship, for whatever reason, fails to live up to the expected quality, the cost of "fixing" a problem is often not limited to just the original defect.

For example, a carpenter sidewalled a house, and installed window and wall flashing incorrectly. Instead of shedding the moisture, the flashing caused water to permeate the wall cavity. For a period of years, water trapped inside caused damage that required the following repairs and replacements:

- *Total windowsill replacement*

- *Replacement of sub-sills and wall framing under the windows*

- *New interior finishes under and around the windows*

Much of the contractor's profit from the original job was lost in time and materials required to make the repairs—all because the flashing was not properly installed. The employee who installed the siding had never been properly instructed on why flashing is used and how it is supposed to perform.

Any problems that are not prevented must be dealt with quickly and efficiently. But the best approach is *not to let problems occur in the first place*. This is done by considering what could go wrong, based on your own previous experience, or on expert information from manufacturers or other authorities.

Documenting and Tracking Defects

Get in the habit of always documenting and tracking the correction of even the smallest defect. Keep detailed records of:

- What the defect is.

- When it was first discovered.

- What its effects are on surrounding work and the overall project.

- Who may be responsible for it (worker, manufacturer, supplier, etc.).

- How the situation was handled, e.g., how the defect was properly corrected.

Common Defect Problems

Be familiar with common defects—problems that frequently occur with construction procedures and materials. For example, if you are finishing a project, and one of the last steps is to paint a concrete wall, it would be helpful to know that manufacturers recommend that concrete be allowed to weather and cure for 30 days prior to painting. This allows the concrete to dry and the alkaline level to recede. Though you may be pressed for time and may be eager to finish up the project, after this waiting period, it is best to test the pH level of the concrete and use an alkali-resistant primer. If you are aware of potential defects from the start, it is much easier to prevent them and/or deal with them if they do occur.

Note: Residential & Light Commercial Construction Standards, published by R.S. Means, is an all-in-one source of guidance and standards from the best-known authorities on the correct installation of everything from concrete and masonry, framing, and finish carpentry/ cabinetry, to insulation, ventilation, roofing and siding, doors and windows, plaster, drywall and tile, ceilings and floor coverings, paint and wall coverings, specialties, plumbing, HVAC, and electrical. This book also lists common defects to look out for in each area of construction. It will help you set standards for subs and employees, answer customers' questions with authority, and check out installation methods for items you haven't worked with before. The book also provides phone numbers and Web site addresses for professional associations and manufacturer product institutes.

Providing Maintenance Program Information

Many problems or deficiencies occur after the project is completed because the property owner has failed to properly care for the space, whether an addition, remodeled area, or new home. Even though the resulting problems are not your fault, the customer may expect you to fix them years after the project has been completed.

One way to avoid these situations is to provide a booklet of maintenance instructions to the client *as soon as the project is complete*. You might even send an annual reminder of necessary tasks, such as changing furnace filters. Some builders use brochures or booklets printed by organizations such as the National Association of Home Builders that explain what homeowners should do to maintain their newly-built homes. *(See the "Resources" section of this book for contact information.)* You could also provide customers with a list of reputable service firms who offer maintenance plans. Be sure to explain to customers exactly what their responsibilities are in caring for their new home or space.

Final Inspection

A thorough final inspection protects all parties—the client, the builder, and the architect (if there is one). If standards of quality were met at every stage of the project, then the final inspection should just reinforce that fact, and there should be no problems. Some of the key checkpoints are listed in Checklist 30. (Note: Professional references such as *Residential & Light Commercial Construction Standards* can be used to add or modify items on this checklist if your region or type of construction calls for more or different requirements.)

Final inspections of remodeling projects have unique concerns that differ from new home construction. If the owner is occupying the space during the work or takes occupancy at substantial completion but before all of the work is finished, it can be more difficult to establish exactly when the job is done. For example, if the owner scratches newly-finished floors while moving furniture, he may not want to accept responsibility and may demand one more coat of finish.

Checkpoints for Final Inspection

Use this checklist to make sure the completed project meets quality standards.

☐ Make sure work conforms to design and contract documents.

Check:

☐ Water infiltration. Recommend water tests to check for leaks (roof, windows, doors).

☐ Site work or preparation:

　☐ To grade.

　☐ Sloping away from building.

　☐ Clean of construction debris.

　☐ Patio and sidewalks free of cracks and heaving.

☐ Drainage away from building.

☐ Landscaping complete and as designed.

　☐ Irrigation system working.

　☐ Plantings and water far enough away from foundation.

　☐ Lawn seeds sprouted, or sod greening.

　☐ Shrubs and trees healthy.

　☐ All original landscaping affected by construction returned to prior condition.

☐ **Roof:**

　☐ Flashing in place.

　☐ Chimney and other penetrations.

☐ Intersection of roof edges and walls.

☐ Gutters and downspouts in place.

☐ Roofing materials installed as per manufacturer's recommendation.

☐ **Attic:**

　☐ Plywood on ceiling joists for storage.

　☐ Insulation in place.

　☐ Electric light in place.

　☐ Properly vented.

☐ **Exterior walls:**

　☐ Weatherstripping in place (doors and windows).

　☐ Flashing and counter-flashing in place.

　☐ Coating (such as stucco) free of cracks. No discoloration.

　☐ Weep holes for water to exit.

　☐ If brick, properly pointed and cleaned.

　☐ Interface between different materials (brick and siding) shows proper alignment without gaps.

　☐ If wood siding, adequate vertical distance between grade and first course of wood shingles or clapboard siding.

Checklist 30

132

Checkpoints for Final Inspection *(continued)*

☐ **Floors: Concrete slabs**

    ☐ Comply with tolerances (e.g., 1/3: in 10').

    ☐ No cracking (except hairline, non-structural).

    ☐ No ponding.

    ☐ Compaction of subgrade test reports and concrete strength test reports on file if required.

☐ **Floors: Wood, Vinyl, Carpet**

    ☐ When walking across:

    ☐ No squeaks.

    ☐ No bouncing or movement.

☐ Vinyl is even, without ridges.

☐ Carpet is stretched tight, showing no seams.

☐ **Walls and ceilings:**

    ☐ Meet standards for gypsum board finish.

    ☐ Show no apparent water marks.

    ☐ Have consistent texture or paint.

    ☐ Have no "thin" spots or "holidays."

    ☐ Match color and texture selected and approved.

    ☐ If suspended ceiling, material is approved per code and fire-rating requirements.

☐ **Windows:** Installed properly including:

    ☐ Flashing.

    ☐ Caulking.

    ☐ Operating properly.

    ☐ No cracks.

    ☐ No air infiltration.

☐ **Doors:**

    ☐ Operating properly.

    ☐ Weatherstripping and flashing in place.

    ☐ Hardware properly installed.

    ☐ Paint or finish as per manufacturer's recommendations.

☐ **Basement walls:**

    ☐ No leaks or dampness.

    ☐ Certificate of waterproofing.

    ☐ No damage apparent to exposed ducts, etc.

    ☐ Firestopping, framing anchors, insulation, and bridging in place.

    ☐ Slab crack-free.

☐ **Fireplaces:**

    ☐ Draft and damper working properly.

Checkpoints for Final Inspection (continued)

- ☐ **HVAC:**
    - ☐ Working properly (balance system).
    - ☐ No hot or cold spots.
    - ☐ Air filters cleaned.
    - ☐ Owner service manuals provided.
- ☐ **Plumbing:**
    - ☐ All fixtures working properly (including showers, toilets, and faucets inside and outside).
- ☐ **Electrical:**
    - ☐ System working properly, including all appliances and outlets.
    - ☐ Garage doors operating properly.
- ☐ **Fire protection system:**
    - ☐ Operating properly.
    - ☐ Power source consistent.

- ☐ **Radon gas venting system in place and functional.**
- ☐ **Obtain:**
    - ☐ Certifications.
    - ☐ Warranties.
    - ☐ Product information.
    - ☐ Final punch list with schedule for completion.
    - ☐ Occupancy permit (if required).

Notes:

_____

_____

_____

_____

_____

Checklist 30

134

Customer Satisfaction

Customer satisfaction surveys can be conducted both during and after the project—as well as after a year or more has passed—to assess long-term quality. A project should aim to meet the customer's requirements while providing the greatest value possible. Simple questionnaires (they could even be anonymous and mailed in by customers) can help establish how the customer feels about the quality of your work, and what you can do to reach a higher level. Use Checklist 31 to receive feedback from customers.

Customers will be happy with the project's quality if:

- Their ideas, concerns, and questions were addressed promptly and thoroughly.
- They were made to feel part of the project and shown individual attention.
- They were kept up-to-date on progress.
- Workmanship was performed well, using appropriate materials, tools and techniques, and skilled craftspeople.
- The final results met or exceeded expectations.

What We Have Learned

Quality is about paying attention to every detail, and performing as required to meet or exceed all of the many necessary standards—contract, building codes and regulations, workmanship, and manufacturers' instructions for product installation. Balancing all of these requirements is part of your responsibility for the total project.

There are so many aspects to quality that it may seem overwhelming to try to master them all. In fact, it's not necessary to take on new or complicated procedures in order to improve your company's quality standards. Quality can be achieved with continued improvements to what you already do—doing better with each project, with each customer, and with each member of your company.

Customer Feedback Questionnaire

Ask customers to fill out the following questionnaire to help you determine the quality of your performance.

Our company is sincerely interested in satisfying our customers. The purpose of this evaluation is for you to tell us how we did, and what, in your opinion, we could do better. You may keep your identity anonymous if you prefer.

	Yes	No

1. Did we fulfill your expectations? How did we or did we not do so? ☐ ☐

Comments: _____

_____

_____

2. Was the work completed on a timely basis? ☐ ☐

Comments: _____

_____

_____

3. Were all of our employees courteous and cooperative? ☐ ☐

Comments: _____

_____

_____

4. Were you satisfied with the cleanup after work was completed? ☐ ☐

Comments: _____

_____

_____

Checklist 31

Customer Feedback Questionnaire *(continued)*

	Yes	No
5. Would you use our company again for future projects?	☐	☐

Comments: _____

_____

_____

| **6.** Would you recommend our company to others? | ☐ | ☐ |

Comments: _____

_____

_____

| **7.** What would you recommend that we do to result in a better job or relationship? | ☐ | ☐ |

Comments _____

_____

_____

Notes:

_____

_____

_____

_____

_____

_____

_____

_____

Checklist 31

Managing Subcontractors

Our Company:

- ☑ Uses only reputable, qualified subcontractors.
- ☑ Treats them fairly.
- ☑ Updates them regularly.
- ☑ Makes sure they meet terms of agreement.
- ☑ Monitors their work.
- ☑ Demands quality work from them.
- ☑ Pays them on a timely basis.

Managing Subcontractors

Unless you can perform all the work on a project on your own, your ability to manage subcontractors plays a big role in your overall success. Your relationships with your subcontractors are one-on-one, contractual relationships. Your duty is to the owner to perform the work set out in your agreement, within the specified time and meeting quality standards. The owner looks only to you, since you have complete responsibility for contract execution and compliance. You are liable if your subcontractors do not perform. Illustration 7.1 shows your stance as the contractor in relation to the owner, subcontractors, and suppliers.

A cooperative relationship with subcontractors should be a high priority. Cooperation makes the work profitable for both of you. Working well together as a team can make projects go more quickly, which makes you more competitive, bringing in more jobs that benefit you both.

How to Manage Subcontractors

The subcontractor is an independent contractor, not your employee. The subcontractor applies his own management skills and expertise to the work he is contracted to perform. You must oversee his job of managing, rather than directly overseeing his crew. This is similar to how an owner oversees a general contractor.

Use Checklist 32 as a guideline for managing subcontractors efficiently.

Fair Treatment

Treating subcontractors fairly includes things like keeping them updated on project details and scheduling, treating them with respect, representing them favorably to the owner, and paying them on time. For example, some contractors make it a policy to pay subcontractors as soon as work is completed—often on the very same day. This can help the project stay on schedule, and can help ensure loyalty and reliable performance on future projects. Other contractors may pay subs according to a schedule, such as weekly or when certain work completion dates are met. The point is to establish some sort of consistency when paying subs, so that they will better be able to manage their own finances and be more willing to work with you in the future.

Use Checklist 33 as a guide for treating subcontractors fairly.

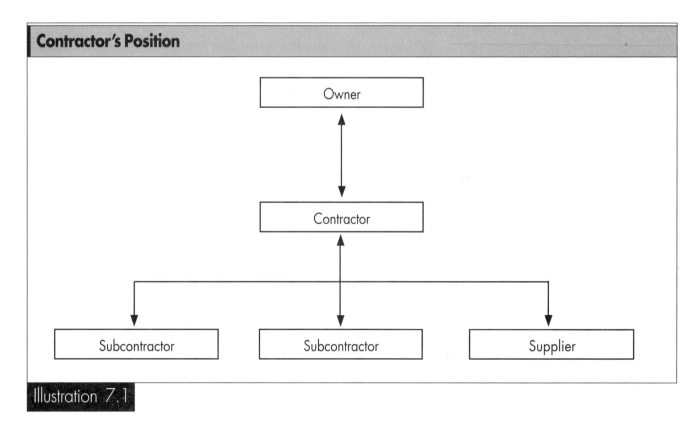

Contractor's Position

Illustration 7.1

How to Manage Subcontractors

Managing subcontractors involves coordinating and overseeing all aspects of the project. You should:

Overall

☐ Select subcontractors who are experienced and qualified, both technically and financially.

☐ Define the job to be done with detail and clarity.

☐ Schedule for performance:

    ☐ Submittals.

    ☐ Milestone dates within the overall schedule.

    ☐ Final completion.

☐ Establish control mechanisms for:

    ☐ Approval of project drawings.

    ☐ Approval of work completed, for progress payments.

☐ Establish requirements for:

    ☐ Quality control.

    ☐ Safety.

    ☐ Written notifications (such as change in scope of work or unforeseen conditions).

☐ Kick off the job with a pre-construction meeting.

☐ Create a team atmosphere.

☐ Answer all project questions completely and as soon as they come up.

☐ Make sure all work complies with contract.

☐ Routinely inspect work to make sure it meets consistent standards.

☐ Pay subcontractors on time for work completed.

How to Manage Subcontractors *(continued)*

Bid Process

☐ Check references to avoid financially weak or unreliable subcontractors.

☐ Become familiar with subcontractors' work.

☐ Work closely with subcontractors to inform them of bid terms and conditions.

Contracting Process

☐ Write a scope of work that fully covers the jobs to be done by subcontractors.

☐ Clarify which trades are to perform which tasks.

☐ Include adequate information regarding product or material samples that will need to be submitted.

☐ Include delivery dates.

Scheduling Process

☐ Include subcontractors' input in original and updated schedules.

☐ Require subcontractors to plan their own work.

☐ Require subcontractors to close out their own work.

☐ Keep subcontractors on schedule.

Notes:

_____

_____

_____

_____

_____

_____

Checklist 32

Treating Subcontractors Fairly

Treating subcontractors fairly helps the project stay on track and helps ensure reliable performance.

☐ Discuss all relevant pre-bid information with subcontractors.

☐ Distribute all requests for estimates to all subcontractors in a timely manner.

☐ Represent subcontractors objectively and fairly to the owner.

☐ Allow subcontractors to participate in change order negotiations.

☐ Keep subcontractors up-to-date on schedule changes.

☐ Pay subcontractors in a timely manner (according to your agreement) for work completed.

Notes:

_____

_____

_____

_____

_____

_____

_____

_____

_____

_____

_____

_____

_____

_____

Checklist 33

Maintaining Relationships

Contractors who have been in the business for a while usually know several subs who do the same kind of work, and often have to choose which particular one to use on a certain job. Sometimes the choice is made for you—only one subcontractor happens to be available to do your job at the required time. Other times you may have to choose between two or three qualified subcontractors, and need to do so without hurting feelings or jeopardizing their future interest in working with you. Maintaining good working relationships with past and present subcontractors can be to your company's advantage, as subs often provide leads for jobs they might be aware of or involved in.

Avoiding Problems

Contractors are responsible for managing subcontractors in these ways:

- Soliciting and accepting bids.

- Qualifying bids.

- Awarding the job.

- Planning and scheduling the work.

- Making sure the work is completed on time and complies with the agreement.

- Effectively communicating, including making daily progress checks.

- Coordinating the work with other parts of the project.

Pricing Subcontracted Work

The process of qualifying subcontractors can be a source of many problems down the road. Some of the disputes that occur during construction could be prevented if more attention had been paid during bidding. Managing subcontractors during bidding includes making sure they:

- Know about contract requirements, such as milestone dates and warranties, and completely understand the scope of work.

- Are aware of site conditions and special requirements of the job.

- Have the opportunity to see all relevant plans and project drawings.

- Bid on all work you expect them to perform.

Knowing the problems and risks of a subcontractor before you sign the contract reduces the chances of discovering them during a crisis halfway through the project. The Subcontract Bid Review in Checklist 34 can help you evaluate subcontractors' bids and select the correct one—not just the lowest one.

However, just because there may be some risks associated with the low-bid subcontractor does not necessarily mean the bid should be rejected. It does mean you should be aware of the problems and figure out in advance how to manage them. Analyzing both the subcontractor's bid and his capability to perform is *risk management*.

The Bid Re-cap Sheet in Illustration 7.2 can help minimize risks during bidding, to make sure that items don't fall through the cracks, and that all subcontractors are bidding on the same items. To create this summary sheet, the following steps must be taken.

Step 1: Read the plans and specifications.

Step 2: Make a list of all items within the subcontractor's scope of work, particularly specialty items or unusual details that subcontractors must include in their bids.

Step 3: Make a bid summary sheet. List all items that must be included in the bid down the side of the sheet. Also include a space for alternates or cost-cutting suggestions. List all expected bidders, as well as a contact person and telephone number, across the top of the page.

Step 4: As bids come in, use this sheet to perform a quick review with the subcontractor. This review will help you make sure that all subcontractors are bidding on the same items. If they have an item in their bid, simply check it off. If not, circle the item. You will have to add a cost for this item during the bid review process. The cost for the missing items can be obtained from the prospective subcontractor, other prospective subcontractors who can give you an idea of the value of the item, or your own estimate.

This process will help you compare subcontractors and decide whether the apparent low bidder is the actual low bidder. Any omitted items will have to be included somewhere and, if not caught in the bid stage, will probably be covered later by a change order, and paid for at a higher rate.

Subcontract Bid Review (Low Bid vs. Correct Bid)

	Yes	No
Has the subcontractor had previous quality problems?	☐	☐
Is he slow to perform work?	☐	☐
Does he resolve problems effectively?	☐	☐
Is he being selected on price alone?	☐	☐
Is he financially sound?	☐	☐
Are there questions about this bid that still need to be resolved?	☐	☐
Is this bid complete?	☐	☐
Can he meet the schedule?	☐	☐
Is it clear what assistance and equipment (crane, scaffolding, storage, etc.) you will provide for this subcontractor?	☐	☐
Does he have proper licenses and insurance?	☐	☐

References:

Company/Customer: Date called: Spoke to:

1. _____

Comments: _____

_____

_____

2. _____

Comments: _____

_____

_____

Checklist 34

CONDENSED BID SUMMARY
SHEET NO. 1/1

PROJECT **SMITH RESIDENCE**
ESTIMATE NO.

LOCATION
TOTAL AREA/VOLUME
DATE

ARCHITECT **ASSOCIATED**
COST PER S.F./C.F.
NO. OF STORIES

BID SECTION : 03 - CONCRETE
EXTENSIONS BY: **FOUNDATION/SLAB**
CHECKED BY:

	ABC CONST.	NORTHWEST	ALLIED	BROWN CONST.	BUDGET
CONTACT	B. SMITH	PAUL JAMES	LINDA S.	SAM B.	
PHONE #	746-2100	781-4130	585-1264	585-8787	
BASE BID	5400	5000	5900	6250	
DOES BASE BID INCLUDE:					
CONCRETE FORMS	✓	✓	✓	✓	3000
ANCHOR BOLTS M&L	✓	No	✓	✓	100
COVER/PROTECT	✓	✓	✓	✓	✓
REBAR MAT.	✓	✓	✓	✓	300
REBAR LABOR	✓	✓	✓	✓	300
DRIVEWAY APPROACH CONC. APRONS	No	No	No	No	500
BASEMENT FLOOR	✓	✓	✓	✓	800
GARAGE FLOOR	✓	✓	✓	✓	600
WALKWAY	No	No	No	No	700
BASEMENT WINDOWS	✓	No	✓	No	200
ALL TAXES, FEES	✓	✓	✓	✓	✓
PERMITS	No	No	No	No	YES
	5400	5000	5900	6250	6500
ADD FOR APRON	500	500	500	500	
ADD FOR WALKWAY	700	700	700	700	
ADD FOR BSMT. WINDOWS	—	200	—	200	
ADD FOR ANCH. BOLTS	—	100	—	—	
	6600	(6500)	7100	7650	6500

OK FOR SCHEDULE. MANPOWER WILL REVIEW # TO CONTRACT FOR $6200.

Illustration 7.2a

149

Bid Re-Cap Sheet: Kitchen Remodel

CONDENSED BID SUMMARY

SHEET NO. _1/1_

PROJECT _SMITH RESIDENCE_

ESTIMATE NO.

LOCATION		TOTAL AREA/VOLUME		DATE	
ARCHITECT _ASSOCIATED_		COST PER S.F./C.F.		NO. OF STORIES	

BID SECTION - KIT. REMODEL   EXTENSIONS BY: _COUNTERS_   CHECKED BY:

	HOME INNOVAT.	SEASIDE	CUSTOM COUNTERS		
CONTACT	BARBARA	VOES.	HANK		
PHONE #	747-1314	781-2086	685-1000		
KITCHEN COUNTER TOP REPLACEMENT					
BASE BID	2500	2750	2125		
DOES BASE BID INCLUDE:					
SPECIFIED MAT.	✓	✓	✓		
LABOR TO REMOVE SINK INSTALL NEW SINK	125 ✓	✓ ✓	125 ✓		
REMOVE TILE @ EXISTING BACK SPLASH	✓	✓	215		
INSTALL NEW BACKSPLASH	✓	✓	✓		
	2625	2750	2465		
SCHEDULE	OK	OK	CANNOT GET ON IT REAL QUICK		
EXPERIENCE ON LAST JOB DONE FOR US	SEVERAL CALL BACKS	EXCELLENT	USED ONCE - POOR CUSTOMER RELATIONS		

Illustration 7.2b

150

Technology such as fax machines and e-mail can speed up the bidding process by instantly confirming bids, and can be used to clarify details—either pre-bid or during construction. When using e-mail for bidding purposes, be sure to file a printed copy.

The Subcontract Agreement

Use these guidelines to prepare and manage the subcontract agreement:

- Clearly describe the scope of work to be performed by the subcontractor. If the subcontractor is to install a total functioning system, state this requirement explicitly.

- Spell out all exceptions to the subcontractor's work in detail. If, for example, you are to perform excavation for the masonry subcontractor, this arrangement should be stated clearly.

- If the subcontractor proposes something different from the original scope of work, resolve the issue and state the work clearly in the contract. Include any requirements for sample materials or products.

- Always have the subcontractor participate in setting up the schedule. This is a key step in promoting the team concept. Include all performance dates. The schedule should be updated when needed, and you should communicate changes to the subcontractor right away.

- Liquidated damages or any other performance penalty should be spelled out in the agreement. Since all previous promises and representations are made null and void by signing the subcontract agreement, spoken warranties and promises that you want to retain as valid should be included in the written agreement. This is where good documentation practices pay off.

- Make sure you cover documents that the subcontractor is required to supply, such as operating instructions, manuals, or warranties.

- *Do not make payment* to any subcontractor who has not signed the contract or has not provided proof of required insurance. In fact, good practice dictates that no subcontractor should be allowed on site without having submitted a valid insurance certificate. You wouldn't want to do business without a detailed contract with the owner, and should not risk subcontracting any portion of the work without a comprehensive signed agreement with an insured subcontractor.

Checklist 35 provides a convenient method for organizing information to include in the agreement and can be used to make sure your own key expectations are included.

Pre-Construction Discussion

Before the beginning of construction, a conversation with all the major subcontractors can set the tone for the job. After that, hold weekly discussions to keep track of progress, coordinate work, and point out potential problems. Checklist 36 lists the topics to be covered in the pre-construction subcontractor conference.

Submittals

If you don't take time to review material samples or product literature, subcontractors could install items that don't meet the owner's expectations or your own quality requirements. (Illustration 5.5 in Chapter 5 is a log to help you keep track of submittals.) If the error is significant, you may have the responsibility of repairing or replacing the item. This situation can also create a negative attitude on the part of the owner, who may scrutinize your every move for the rest of the job. The owner's approval of a product, or your approval of materials, should be documented.

Coordinate and Cooperate

You must plan the schedule and coordinate progress so that each subcontractor can work efficiently and without unreasonable interference from other subcontractors. You also need to ensure quality assurance, handle any backcharges, and manage any changes or extras. If you don't coordinate and ensure cooperation, you invite subcontractors to increase their fees for doing work out of sequence, and/or justify a delay in their work.

Throughout the project, be sure to maintain your proper stance between the owner and subcontractors, acting as intermediary and maintaining control of the project. To stay in the middle, follow the guidelines in Checklist 37.

To ensure cooperation, you must make sure that all work is properly performed and all appropriate preparations are made by the time each subcontractor moves into an area. This is what is called a "state of readiness." Checklist 38, Site Preparation, will help. As part of the responsibility to coordinate and cooperate, you may have to inform a subcontractor who is behind schedule of the need to catch up.

Subcontract Agreement

Use this checklist to determine if your written subcontract agreement is complete.

Does the subcontract contain:

	Yes	No	Date
An adequate work statement?	☐	☐	_____
A list of all specifics included in the contract?	☐	☐	_____
A list of all exclusions of the work to be performed or material to be furnished?	☐	☐	_____
A schedule for performance?	☐	☐	_____
Safety responsibilities?	☐	☐	_____
Long lead-time requirements?	☐	☐	_____
Spoken agreements (with backup documentation)?	☐	☐	_____
Taxes (if any) included in price?	☐	☐	_____
Protection of work in place and stored materials?	☐	☐	_____
Layout requirements?	☐	☐	_____
Cleanup requirements?	☐	☐	_____
Insurance requirements? Certificates on file?	☐	☐	_____
Specific or unusual warranty provisions?	☐	☐	_____
Method and terms of payments?	☐	☐	_____
Description of paperwork required for final payment?	☐	☐	_____
Has a signed copy of the agreement without exceptions or conditions been returned to your office?	☐	☐	_____

Checklist 35

Pre-Construction Subcontractor Conference

The typical pre-construction conference should cover the following topics:

☐ Safety.

☐ The project schedule.

☐ Performance standards review.

☐ Subcontractors' relationship with owner and inspectors.

☐ Importance of communicating existing and potential problems.

☐ How to maintain proper records, such as daily reports and accident reports.

☐ Quality assurance requirements for quality control.

☐ Material handling plan (storage, lifts, cranes, etc.).

☐ Payment procedures.

Notes:

_____

_____

_____

_____

_____

_____

_____

_____

_____

_____

_____

Checklist 36

Guidelines for the Contractor

To properly maintain your contractual role, follow these basic guidelines:

☐ Don't allow the owner to deal directly with subcontractors without your permission.

☐ Get the owner's interpretation on scope of work disputes and then pass them on to subcontractors.

☐ If the owner has a problem with subcontractor (or his work), let the subcontractor know.

☐ Give subcontractors a chance to present their views on inspection disputes.

☐ Don't sign off completely on change orders unless affected subcontractors have also reviewed and signed off on the work involved.

Notes:

_____

_____

_____

_____

_____

_____

_____

_____

_____

_____

_____

Checklist 37

Site Preparation

Part of coordinating subcontractors is getting a work area ready. You should make reasonable attempts to:

☐ Provide access to the workplace on a timely basis.

☐ Make sure the space (such as a concrete slab for a framing contractor) is complete and meets the correct tolerances to accept the work.

☐ Make sure any equipment or materials furnished by other subcontractors (such as recessed light fixture units in the case of a drywall contractor) are delivered and installed on a timely basis.

☐ Make sure environmental conditions (such as temperature and humidity in the building) are in accordance with accepted standards.

☐ Make sure that other trades are not working in conflict with subcontractors.

☐ Make sure all inspections are complete prior to the beginning of the next trade.

Notes:

_____

_____

_____

_____

_____

_____

_____

_____

_____

_____

_____

Checklist 38

Quality Assurance

Checking subcontractors' work cannot be emphasized enough. If a subcontractor installs a portion of the job that later fails and causes injury or other damage, you may be held liable. In cases where general contractors were unable to show proof that subcontractors' work met with the project's contract requirements, several lawsuits have been decided against the general contractor. And, of course, such situations can be damaging to your reputation. You may also wind up footing the bill for rework or paying for an extension of the job.

It is up to you to set quality control procedures to make sure that subcontractors' work meets the requirements. If you have a written agreement, it may allow you to take over a subcontractor's work if he is not making satisfactory progress after three days (from the time a written notice is issued). *(See Chapter 6 for more on Quality Control.)*

Backcharges

As stated earlier, you should, as a matter of policy, try to maintain a firm, but cooperative relationship with subcontractors. If you are unreasonably demanding, you will eventually suffer for these actions. If a subcontractor fails to perform part of a contractual obligation (such as cleanup or completing a punch list), you may reserve the right to "backcharge" him for the cost associated with completing the work for him. However, backcharging should be the exception rather than the rule. Where a real backcharge item does exist, the cost should be properly documented, and the situation clearly explained to the subcontractor.

Changes and Extras

All changes and extra work that you ask a subcontractor to perform should be in the form of a written Work Authorization. If you don't put these things in writing, you can quickly lose control of a project. The sources and/or reasons for changes can be forgotten if they are not documented properly. The scope of the work should be clearly stated in the work authorization, including labor-hours, materials, and equipment. You should negotiate a lump sum price for the extra work before it is performed. *(See Chapter 4 for more on lump sum and other types of contracts.)*

Work authorization directives are issued to subcontractors for three reasons:

- Item(s) are left out of the initial subcontract agreement.
- Changeorders are issued by the owner.
- On-site incidents occur, such as storms or accidents.

You should always negotiate for a reasonable price before allowing the subcontractor to proceed with work not in the original subcontract agreement. If the subcontractor will not agree to a reasonable price, you should have another option available.

Project Close-out

The last part of the project is often the most difficult to manage. By this point, subcontractors may be sharing space with finish carpenters; materials may be in short supply; and tools and equipment may be in demand on another job. The close-out phase of a project must be managed as if it were a new job just beginning. To properly manage subcontractors during close-out, you should follow the guidelines in Checklist 39.

Subcontractor Evaluation

The performance of subcontractors should be reviewed periodically. You should be able to objectively assess their work to use as a negotiating tool on a future job and to encourage an upgrade in quality. Relying on "gut feelings" may put too much emphasis on quick observations or memory. It's a good idea to get into the habit of keeping a written file (formal or informal) of your objective evaluation—recorded both after the project is complete and as you encounter issues along the way. (Some of the questions in Checklist 34 could be used as a starting point for this purpose.)

What We Have Learned

The operative word in subcontractor management is *management*, which includes selecting qualified subcontractors and knowing and doing something about the risks associated with a particular subcontractor. Your job includes establishing a clear scope of work, and verifying that bids include the full scope of work. Once the job is underway, managing subcontractors is essential to maintaining a team atmosphere. By coordinating and monitoring the work of all subs and demanding that work meets your standards of quality and the requirements of the agreement, your project will be successful.

Remember, most legal problems on construction projects are due to a management failure by someone—don't let it be you!

Project Close-out

To properly manage subcontractors during project close-out, you should:

☐ Update the schedule often and re-plan the final weeks, bringing subcontractors into the scheduling process.

☐ Prepare and oversee completion of a preliminary punch list before each subcontractor leaves the project.

☐ Send notification to subcontractors informing them of data requirements (operating or maintenance manuals, brochures, as-built drawings, warranties, waivers of lien, etc.), and that final payment will be withheld if that data is not submitted.

☐ Coordinate all required final inspections and sign off with subcontractors and regulatory agencies.

☐ Tie up all loose ends. Backcharges and change orders should be negotiated while key people are still available and while the details are still fresh in their minds.

Notes:

_____

_____

_____

_____

_____

_____

_____

_____

_____

_____

_____

Checklist 39

Creating Reliable Estimates

Our Company:

☑ Has an organized approach to estimating.

☑ Makes adequate site visits before estimating.

☑ Considers unknowns and risks (such as concealed conditions), either by including a contingency or by special conditions in the contract.

☑ Captures all overhead costs.

☑ Knows market conditions (e.g., availability of labor and materials and the competition).

☑ Has a job cost system for collecting historical data.

Creating Reliable Estimates

The purpose of an estimate is to calculate as closely as possible the expected costs of labor, materials, and equipment, allowing for a reasonable profit. Accurate cost estimates—for both remodeling and new construction projects—are essential to your company's success.

Each estimate is both a mathematical exercise and a business judgment call. It's mathematical because you need to calculate how much it will cost to do the work. It's a judgment call because you need to decide what it will take to win the job, and how much you want it.

Estimating materials, equipment, labor, and overhead may in some cases be easier than making the judgment call on the profit and bid price. And an accurate estimate is vital. There are countless examples of contractors losing money because of estimating errors, or because they did not fully review the plans or understand the scope of work. Contractors can lose money if they fail to visit and inspect the site adequately before estimating, if they don't consider concealed conditions, or if they underestimate the necessary labor or time. The estimate is one of the most important things you do, and one that demands quality control.

Determining what it takes to get the job may not be as clear-cut. It may be a matter of price. For example, the customer may already have a quote that is lower than yours. The competition may be willing to take the project for hardly any mark-up, or an inexperienced builder may underbid the job. You may also find that you have been consistently high on your bids lately because you are not bidding to market conditions, or your overhead has crept up to a point where it's tough to be competitive. Or another construction company, even with a higher bid, may get a job because they are better known to the customer.

So, in addition to doing an estimate of what the job will cost, you'll need to do an analysis of what it will take to get the job. Counting materials and putting an accurate price on them is crucial, but may not be enough to get the work. Always think in terms of customers and what it will take to motivate them to purchase the work from your company. It may be quality of workmanship, speed, reliability, or known reputation in the community.

Putting together an estimate can mean many long hours of hard work, with no certainty of getting the job. But it can also mean an opportunity to gain profitable work. Larger contractors may bid ten or more jobs in order to win just one. Their success often depends on having a system in place to prepare estimates in an accurate, organized way.

Reviewing the Specifications

The first step before starting the estimate is to obtain copies of the plans and/or specifications/project description (scope of work). Make extra copies so you can mark them up with notes. During the first review of the specifications, identify and note all items to be priced. Check all work to be subcontracted and "related work" requirements from other trades. Evaluate the various parts of the project to determine which areas need the most attention. When you are familiar with the specifications, ask subcontractors and vendors for their prices. *(See Chapter 7 for more on pricing subcontracted work.)*

If an architect is involved, there may be a pre-bid meeting for bidding contractors. These meetings can be very helpful, as important points may be brought up and details clarified. Attending also shows that you are interested in the project, and helps to ensure that everyone is bidding on the same things. Carefully review the plans and specifications to become as familiar as possible with the project beforehand.

Scope of Work

The scope of work must specify clearly not only the construction to be performed, but also the quality of materials, fixtures, and finishes (and which materials will be supplied by the owner), and who (your workforce or the owner's) will perform the various parts of the work.

The scope of work must also include peripheral items that may cost you, including:

- Insurance
- Permits
- Surveying certifications (required by the lender for items like foundation layout)
- Architect/engineer review/stamp on plans
- Temporary facilities
- Temporary power
- Storage
- Site security and/or protection
- Traffic control

The quantity and quality of material should be defined by the scope of work (or specifications). Properly done, this is the non-variable portion of the estimate. If you know how much drywall will be involved, for example, you'll find out how much it costs per sheet or square foot, and you can pin this price down with certainty. *(See Chapter 4 for more on scope of work.)*

Site Visit

To create a reliable estimate for any project, you must visit and evaluate the site (often several times). This is particularly important for repair and remodeling jobs where you need to become familiar with the existing conditions, the unique requirements of the project, and possible risks associated with hidden conditions. Before conducting a visit, make sure to thoroughly review the plans, if available. If possible, subcontractors should visit the site with you to gain a better understanding of the required work and site conditions.

Pre-bid investigation relates to all potential conditions that can affect the work, including:

- Weather conditions
- Labor supply
- Material availability
- Utilities
- Potential safety issues

When visiting the site, examine every detail thoroughly, taking notes and photographs. In a remodeling project, an error or oversight can have a huge effect on the accuracy of the estimate. It can even mean using a different method of construction than the one you planned and estimated. Verify dimensions and constructability of the new project, and be familiar with the types of construction and materials in the existing building.

During the visit, your past experience and knowledge will help you identify requirements or potential problems that may not have been included in the plans or project description. Make sure that the work is clearly defined for each subcontractor so they won't overlap. This type of misunderstanding often occurs on remodeling jobs.

The best way to evaluate and analyze an existing structure is from the bottom up. By beginning the inspection of existing conditions at the foundation, you can review the structure in the order it was built and identify and follow building systems up through the structure. The mechanical/piping and electrical systems, for example, can be traced from below to better understand the distribution above.

When visiting and evaluating the site, consider:

- How will delivered materials be stored and protected?
- Are there any obstacles to material handling?
- How will adjacent areas be protected from dust and general disturbances?
- What are the limitations on equipment usage? (e.g., site access, noise restrictions)
- What demolition will be required?

During the site visit, take notes on potential risks. Risks have a direct correlation to labor costs. If the project is a remodeling job and much of the area is overhead (piping, conduits, etc.), it may be impossible to conduct a complete survey of all the hidden conditions. The homeowner will want you to assume the risk of conditions that can increase the cost, but cannot be fully investigated in a pre-bid site investigation. If the risk is significant, you may need to add contingencies to your labor budget or figure out another way to deal with unforeseeable conditions. Perhaps you'll become the low bidder in the process. Checklist 41 lists items you should be sure to check during the site visit.

Developing the Estimate

A thorough estimate addresses all of these related factors:

- Quantity of materials and equipment
- Quality of materials and equipment
- Job conditions [including addressing the season and weather (cold, rainy, etc.)]
- Availability and quality of labor force
- Availability and quality of supervision
- Duration of the job and how tight the schedule is
- The amount of overhead directly related to running the job
- The amount of home office overhead being allocated to the job
- A reasonable profit

Use Checklist 40 to make sure your estimate addresses all of these issues.

After the contract has been awarded, a complete and accurate estimate is a helpful tool for construction planning. While different contractors use different estimating methods, most follow a plan like this:

- Prepare a quantity survey.
- Divide the work into individual items.
- Obtain unit prices for each item, and calculate the cost of that item multiplied by the number required.
- Arrange the estimate into the appropriate format for bid or submittal.

Checklist 41 lists all the steps in the estimating process in detail.

The final estimate must include not only the "hard costs"—materials and labor needed to produce the finished product, but also the "soft costs" required for performing the work. Soft costs include:

- Overhead and main office expenses.
- Profit.
- Insurance.
- Testing costs (such as soil compaction).
- Temporary requirements (such as scaffolding, shoring, dumpster rental, or portable toilets).
- Equipment (such as hoisting equipment).

Elements of the Estimate

Use this checklist to make sure you address each aspect of estimating. All estimates should include:

☐ Material quantity and quality.

☐ Equipment quantity and quality.

☐ Labor needed to install the material.

☐ Job duration and schedule requirements.

☐ Price of subcontractors' work.

☐ Costs of:

    ☐ Insurance, bonds.

    ☐ Permits.

    ☐ Site protection (drainage, berms).

    ☐ Safety (such as barricades).

    ☐ Home office overhead.

    ☐ Other general conditions.

☐ Costs of all items affected by time:

    ☐ Supervision.

    ☐ Truck rental.

    ☐ Dumpster rental.

    ☐ Equipment.

    ☐ Cost increases.

    ☐ Financing (interest).

☐ A reasonable profit (and still be competitive!).

Checklist 40

Estimating Tasks

Use this checklist to make sure you address all steps in the estimating process.

☐ Get the plans and specifications (or scope of work) and make sure you thoroughly understand the requirements to be priced.

☐ Identify the items you will perform and those that will be subbed out.

☐ Consult the architect or owner on any unclear items.

☐ Visit the site.

  ☐ Become familiar with existing conditions.

  ☐ Look for hidden or concealed risks.

  ☐ Check out all dimensions (on remodel of older buildings, for example, you may find that window opening dimensions and floor-to-ceiling heights vary).

  ☐ Find out about interference with work, due to access limitations or the owner's presence.

  ☐ Determine any limitations on use of existing building facilities (such as an elevator).

  ☐ Check out storage and material handling availability.

  ☐ Check out power availability.

  ☐ Determine whether any hazards exist on the site (such as lead paint, asbestos, or underground fuel tanks) and how they must be dealt with.

  ☐ Determine any limitations on equipment use.

☐ Consider only qualified subcontractors and reliable suppliers.

☐ Obtain subcontractor and supplier quotes.

☐ Keep a separate file for quotes.

☐ Review quotes carefully to make sure they include all necessary items. If not, ask subs to revise them.

☐ Do a material takeoff (count quantities, including waste).

☐ Determine what discounts you can receive for buying in bulk or making timely payments.

Checklist 41

Estimating Tasks (continued)

- ☐ Determine which items have a long lead time and must be ordered early. Late delivery could impact productivity.

- ☐ Determine if you already have some materials in stock (re-bar, 2 x 4s, etc.) that have been paid for and charged out on other jobs.

- ☐ Determine if there are any items that can be pre-fabricated or shop-built to reduce field labor installation (such as roof joists, custom millwork, and finishing pre-hung doors).

- ☐ Determine whether you will have to submit material samples to the architect for approval. (The more submittals required, the more project management time will be needed, which may affect overhead costs.)

- ☐ Determine labor costs.

- ☐ Determine "general conditions" or other direct costs, including:

  - ☐ Bond.

  - ☐ Insurance.

  - ☐ Permits.

  - ☐ Safety.

  - ☐ Ice and water for personnel.

  - ☐ Toilet facilities.

  - ☐ Temporary power and other utilities.

  - ☐ On-site trailer, if applicable.

  - ☐ Telephone and other communication.

  - ☐ Transportation of personnel.

  - ☐ Temporary protection and security.

Checklist 41

• Weather or time-sensitive costs.

These items can add up to a large percentage of the total project cost.

The importance of accurately estimating the quantity of materials to be installed (including allowances for waste) cannot be stressed enough. If you don't have enough materials delivered and available, you may risk losing your labor forces, who may leave the job to do other work.

Unit Price Estimate

The *unit price estimate* is the most accurate and detailed of the estimate types, and takes the most time to complete. All decisions about building materials and methods must be made before preparing a unit price estimate. You should consult the working drawings and specifications (or the contract's project description), perform necessary site visits, and plan how you will do the work. The unit price estimate is used primarily for bidding purposes, and should have an accuracy of plus or minus no more than five percent.

A unit price estimate is sometimes referred to as a *trade estimate* or *product classification estimate*, which means that when preparing the estimate, builders focus on building materials and the trades involved with actual installation. A recommended system for organizing unit price estimates is the CSI MasterFormat with its 16 divisions that cover everything from general requirements and excavation to finish work, plumbing, and electrical. The CSI standard is widely used in the construction industry.

Before assigning unit costs, you need to first identify the materials needed to complete the project and the time needed to install them. The time is based on the total hours of the people who will be working on the job and the equipment needed for each specific task. Duration of equipment use must be noted to account for time-related costs, such as rental and operator fees, fuel, and (if you own the equipment) wear and tear—a depreciation item on your taxes. Your job is to designate a unit of measure, determine the quantity of units, and establish a reasonable cost per unit.

There are many information sources available to help you with your estimate. The most dependable figures are current prices and bids from suppliers and subs, along with your own actual costs for similar, recent projects. An up-to-date industry cost book, such as R.S. Means *Contractor's Pricing Guides*, can also be helpful. The

Contractor's Pricing Guides, updated annually, contain residential detailed costs and framing and rough carpentry costs with factors that let you adjust for your own locality. The books describe the type of work to be performed, the appropriate crew, and the time needed to perform the work, and provide separate costs for materials, labor, and equipment. Total costs are extended to include overhead and profit. (Another Means publication, *Plan Reading & Material Takeoff*, explains and illustrates the entire quantity takeoff process—from excavation and paving, through framing, roofing and siding, mechanical/electrical, interior finishes, and site work—for residential and light commercial projects.)

You may also find estimating software helpful. *CostWorks* is the electronic version of R.S. Means' *Residential Construction Cost Data*, and includes all the same cost information plus additional features, such as automatic adjustment to your location and calculation of quantities to line items. Data and estimates can be exported to a spreadsheet.

When the quantities have been counted, values in the form of unit costs are applied, and markups (such as overhead and profit) are added in order to come up with the total "selling price," or the quote.

Square Foot Estimate

Square foot estimates are often used before plans and specifications are prepared, when the budget is first being established. As with unit price estimates, the best source of square foot costs is your own cost records for similar projects, which can then be adjusted to the project at hand. Another source is R.S. Means annual *Contractor's Pricing Guide: Residential Square Foot Costs*.

Labor

Labor required to install materials is the most variable part of the estimate, and the cost category that contractors tend to have the most trouble with. Labor is based on:

- Your historical costs (what it has cost you to do this type of work on other recent projects).
- Your commitment to job site planning.
- Quality of supervision.
- Quality and availability of craftsmen.
- Duration of the job (and how much overtime will be required).

- Job conditions (including available workspace and if other trades will be working in the same space at the same time).

- The effects of weather or season (cold or hot, damp or dry) on various tasks.

- Your experience and expected level of quality. [This is the reason to keep track of the cost of re-work on your jobs. You may know what your jobs should cost (your original estimate), but you must know what they are really costing you and why. All good estimators keep a record of actual job costs.]

- What kind of turnover you've been having. If it has been high, expect labor costs to be higher. If you use a core of trained, permanent workers, your productivity will be better.

History shows that some contractors have a difficult time controlling their labor budget, even (and maybe especially) on small projects with fast turn-around. Investment in hiring and training qualified personnel generally pays off in improved overall labor costs and a better quality of workmanship.

Some suggestions to accurately estimate labor:

- Get input from your field supervisor if you have one.

- Refer to pricing guides (such as R.S. Means *Contractor Pricing Guides*) to get a benchmark.

- Use your own labor costs based on similar, recent work in the past.

- For each item of work, figure the size crew it will take for:
  - Material handling.
  - Installation (including related items like pointing and patching).
  - Cleanup.

You should also consider the make-up of the crew and determine if you can you use apprentices to do material handling and cleanup in order to reduce labor costs. Be sure to consider obstacles such as weather, site access limitations, and other activities that may be going on at the same time in the building. Also address:

- What tools and equipment will be needed and the rental or other costs associated with them.

- The standard replacement rate of small tools.

- If equipment (such as backhoes) will be rented. If owned, what standard charges should you include in the estimate? If this equipment has already been paid for and depreciated, you might consider reducing the amount you normally charge for it in your estimate.

- The experience of your crew and supervisor(s). Experienced workers are more cost effective due to their ability to produce quality workmanship on a timely basis.

Overhead and Profit

Overhead

Because an estimate is an educated guess of what it will cost your company to complete a project, it must include all items that have a cost, including both field and home office overhead. The home office overhead must provide for payment of interest on debt and all other expenses, such as office rent and utilities, insurance, and accounting costs, whether or not payments for these items are made during the project's time frame.

The overhead portion of your estimate can be used as a snapshot of how well you are managed and how competitive you can be. If your overhead is high, your bid price may be higher than your competitors'. If your injury incidence is high, your overhead is likely to be high because your insurance premiums will be higher. If productivity in the field is poor, if you have a lot of turnover, or if workmanship has to be redone, your schedule may run over, which may extend your overhead costs beyond what you had budgeted. If your estimate does not consider these factors and you get the job, you may very well lose money.

Profit

In addition to covering your home office overhead, you must include a reasonable profit in your bid price. While a home office is a real cost that you can identify and recover (through a percentage of the direct costs of doing the work), profit is a decision you might make on a case-by-case basis. You may wish to reduce the profit to make sure you are going to acquire a particular job, or increase it if the project is higher-risk (using higher profit as a bit of a contingency). This is all part of determining the "mark-up" each job carries.

The Decision to Bid

One of the most important decisions you make is whether or not to bid a job. Smart contractors are selective in the jobs they bid. They check out the credit of prospective customers, make sure they have capable workers available at the time, and make sure that the project is within their area of competence. You should also make sure you have enough cash flow available for the job. Before you jump into the bid, carefully consider whether you should pursue this project.

The estimating phase for both large and small contractors can be time-consuming and costly. Many contractors get only about ten percent of the jobs they go after. Using the pre-qualification process (decision to bid) may help you improve your ratio. Also, getting to know the priorities of potential customers (are they most interested in a reasonable price, speed, highest quality, or your ability to work without disrupting the household?) may give you an edge if you are able to respond to their real needs.

Developing Winning Proposals

The customer, as previously indicated, may be most interested in a low price, or there may be other factors that will sway his choice of one builder over others. If their priority is to get the job done quickly, you may want to include in your proposal the steps you will take to deliver the project to meet the customer's schedule requirements. If a customer is concerned with your ability to work cooperatively with existing operations of their household or business, then you should address this in the proposal. Checklist 42 is a list of items you may want to include in your proposal to help show the customer your particular qualifications.

One of the key reasons for disputes between builders and customers (or potential customers) is that they don't see eye to eye on scope and quality. It often helps to walk the customer through your estimate. An "open book" approach with customers provides understanding and builds trust. You many need to assess each customer and circumstance to decide if this is the right approach for the project.

What We Have Learned

An estimate must not only correctly count and price all the needed labor, materials, and equipment for a job, but also consider *site conditions* and *market conditions*. A good estimator identifies risks of unknown conditions and either assigns a price to them or includes a limitation on the extent of work in the contract—or figures out a way to manage the risks so that all costs are controlled.

Small-volume contractors in particular must make sure their estimates are correct and that customers know what is and isn't included in the bid price. For example, if you are changing out bathroom fixtures, are you to repaint the entire wall or just touch up

Developing a Winning Proposal

The key to developing a winning proposal is to include accurate and thorough information about your company, and address any issues that may be of particular concern to the customer. Include the following items in your proposal.

☐ Your company's experience (and references).

☐ Financial integrity (and banking references) of your company.

☐ The qualifications and experience of your supervisory personnel.

☐ The competence of your subcontractors.

☐ A detailed worksheet or checklist that itemizes by room or structure the work to be done.

☐ What value your company brings to this project and how you will address the customer's concerns (based on your visits and conversations with the customer).

☐ Your awareness of factors, such as noise and dust and measures to control them.

☐ Options the customer may wish to consider.

☐ Your ability to meet the schedule requirements.

☐ Your willingness (if you are willing) to have an "open book" examination of your costs.

☐ Your commitment to quality.

☐ Your commitment to cleanup after the project is complete.

☐ Your desire for the customer to evaluate your company's performance when the work is complete.

Notes:

_____

_____

_____

_____

Checklist 42

the portion that is damaged? If you discover rotting sheathing during window replacement, how will the extra cost for this unplanned work be covered? Were these issues included in your estimate? What, if any, exclusions did you specify in the contract? The proposal should clearly spell these things out, for your benefit and the customer's.

The following is the equation of successful, customer-driven builders.

Sales Pitch (work promised) = Estimate (complete and accurate) = Contract = Performance

Estimating is the critical second step in the evolution of a successful project.

Resources

The following is a list of associations and Web sites that can be valuable for builders and remodelers. They provide information on building codes and standards, safety, products and suppliers, industry updates, certification and education, business management, and technology developments.

Professional Career and Development Associations

ABC: Associated Builders and Contractors
1300 N. Seventeenth Street
Suite 800
Rosslyn, VA 22209
703-812-2000
http://www.abc.org

ABC is a national trade association for contractors, subcontractors, and suppliers. With over 80 local chapters, it offers educational and safety training (including a partnership program with OSHA), as well as resources for managing your business, such as insurance services information and a guide to public relations. The Web site provides industry links and updates.

AGC: The Associated General Contractors of America
333 John Carlyle Street
Suite 200
Alexandria, VA 22314
703-548-3118
http://www.agc.org

AGC is one of the nation's largest trade associations. It has 100 chapters throughout the country and offers industry updates, educational opportunities, safety information, and publications. The Web site also offers information on obtaining contract documents, legislation, and an extensive marketplace for communicating with companies including material and equipment suppliers, financial services, consultants, and technology providers.

AIA: The American Institute of Architects
1735 New York Avenue, NW
Washington, DC 20006
202-626-7300
http://www.aiaonline.com

AIA offers contract documents, a listing of architects, technical publications, and other professional resources.

ASA: American Subcontractors Association
1004 Duke Street
Alexandria, VA 22314
703-684-3450
http://www.asaonline.com

ASA is a trade association for subcontractors, specialty trade contractors, and suppliers. Its Web site offers industry updates, product and supplier information, legislative reports, and other resources.

ASPE: American Society of Professional Estimators
11141 Georgia Avenue
Suite #412
Wheaton, MD 20902
301-929-8848
http://www.aspenational.com

ASPE offers a certification program, continuing education, and employment opportunities for construction estimators.

CFMA: Construction Financial Management Association
29 Emmons Drive
Suite F-50
Princeton, NJ 08540
609-452-8000
http://www.cfma.org

CFMA offers financial management education and information for contractors, subcontractors, architects, engineers, and suppliers. Its site offers job postings, a buyer's guide for computer software, workshops on topics such as construction accounting, and other resources.

HBI: Home Builder's Institute
1090 Vermont Avenue, NW
Suite 600
Washington, DC 20005
(202) 371-0600
http://www.hbi.org

HBI is the official educational branch of NAHB and offers training, job placement, continuing education, and apprenticeship programs.

NAHB: National Association of Home Builders
1201 15th Street, NW
Washington, DC 20005-2800
800-368-5242
http://www.nahb.org

NAHB, consisting of more than 800 local builders' associations, provides builders with industry updates, including information on safety and regulations, construction techniques and tips, design ideas, and business management and educational resources. The National Association of Home Builders Research Center, a subsidiary of NAHB, tests and certifies building products and new technologies, maintains building codes and standards, and trains trades on new construction techniques and materials.

NARI: National Association of the Remodeling Industry
780 Lee Street
Suite 200
Des Plaines, IL 60016
847-298-9200
http://www.nari.org

NARI's members are remodeling contractors and subcontractors, manufacturers, suppliers, lenders, and others. It offers education and technical information for both professionals and homeowners. NARI's certification program includes designations as Certified Remodeler and Certified Lead Carpenter and establishes quality standards for remodeling practices. NARI's Web site offers contractor referrals, publications, and educational programs.

NAWIC: National Association of Women in Construction
327 South Adams Street
Fort Worth, TX 76104
817-877-5551
http://www.nawic.org

NAWIC represents women in construction, including business owners, managers, and trade workers, and has partnerships with a number of other associations, including the American Subcontractors Association, the Associated Builders and Contractors, and Associated General Contractors of America. Its educational programs include courses in CAD, document specialist, and construction basics.

The Trades

ASCC: American Society of Concrete Contractors
38800 Country Club Drive
Farmington Hills, MI 48331
800-877-2753
http://www.ascconc.org

ASCC represents concrete contractors. Its Web site offers solutions to concrete problems and allows you to submit questions. The site also lists suppliers in your region and offers publications and articles.

AWCI: Association of the Wall & Ceiling Industries International
803 West Broad Street
Suite 600
Falls Church, VA 22046
703-534-8300
http://www.awci.org

AWCI members are wall and ceiling contractors, product suppliers, and product manufacturers, including those who work with acoustical, drywall, exterior insulation and finishing, fireproofing, flooring, and stucco materials and systems. The Web site offers technical and product information and educational seminars.

AWI: Architectural Woodworking Institute
1952 Isaac Newton Square
Reston, VA 20190
703-733-0600
http://www.awinet.org

AWI provides woodworkers with industry updates, training and certification, and listings of woodworkers and suppliers. The organization also sets woodworking standards and offers publications on such topics as achieving quality standards and finishing woodwork.

IEC: Independent Electrical Contractors
2010-A Eisenhower Avenue
Alexandria, VA 22314
703-549-7351
http://www.ieci.org

IEC's members are independent electrical contractors. The organization offers training programs recognized by the U.S. Department of Labor's Bureau of Apprenticeship and Training. Its Web site offers technical information and publications, industry updates, and other resources.

MCAA: Mechanical Contractors Association of America
1385 Piccard Drive
Rockville, MD 20850
301-869-5800
http://www.mcaa.org

MCAA offers contractors a searchable network of mechanical, plumbing, and service contractors, industry updates, and courses and seminars on topics such as estimating and management skills. Its Web site provides industry news including technology developments and regulatory changes, as well as publications and product information.

NFBA: National Frame Builders Association
4840 West 15th Street
Suite 1000
Lawrence, KS 66049
800-557-6957
http://www.postframe.org

NFBA represents post-frame constructors, manufacturers, and code developers. Its Web site offers a referral service, product and supplier locators, and business and technical information and publications.

NRCA: National Roofing Contractors Association
10255 W. Higgins Road
Suite 600
Rosemont, IL 60018
800-323-9545
http://www.nrca.net

NRCA is a professional association for roofing contractors, as well as architects, engineers, manufacturers, and distributors. NRCA is affiliated with over 100 local, state, and international roofing contractor associations. Its Web site offers technical information, product and distributor locators, industry updates, and education.

PDCA: Painting & Decorating Contractors of America
3913 Old Lee Highway
Suite 33B
Fairfax, VA 22030
800-332-PDCA
http://www.pdca.com

PDCA represents painting and decorating contractors. It maintains professional standards for coating systems, touch-up painting and damage repair, and job sequencing. PDCA provides certification and up-to-date information on products and research information.

Product Manufacturers

BIA: The Brick Institute of America
11490 Commerce Park Drive
Reston, VA 20191
703-620-0100
http://www.bia.org

BIA offers technical information, courses, and product information for residential and commercial builders and designers, as well as homeowners. Their interactive Web site provides answers to common brick installation and maintenance questions, code updates, new product information, photo galleries, and design ideas.

CRI: The Carpet and Rug Institute
P.O. Box 2048
Dalton, GA 30722
800-882-8846
http://www.carpet-rug.com

CRI is a national trade association whose Web site offers technical information useful to both builders and homeowners, including floor covering installation methods, advice, and tips; industry standards;

lists of certified installers and retailers; and selection and maintenance information.

DHI: Door and Hardware Institute
14150 Newbrook Drive
Suite 200
Chantilly, VA 20151
703-222-2010
http://www.dhi.org

DHI is a professional organization providing education and information about doors, hardware, and specialty products for manufacturers, distributors, architects, and contractors. Its Web site offers a buyer's guide for products and manufacturers, educational programs on topics such as architectural hardware and security doors, technical handbooks, and other resources.

KCMA: Kitchen Cabinet Manufacturers Association
1899 Preston White Drive
Reston, VA 20191
703-264-1690
http://kcma.org

KCMA is a trade association for manufacturers and suppliers of kitchen and bathroom cabinets and countertops. KCMA maintains voluntary performance standards (ANSI/KCMA A161.1). Its Web site offers searchable listings of products and suppliers, certification, training, and industry updates.

NKBA: National Kitchen and Bath Association
687 Willow Grove St.
Hackettstown, NJ 07840
908-852-0033
http://www.nkba.org

NKBA represents kitchen and bath installers, product manufacturers, and suppliers and has over 50 local chapters. Its Web site offers professional development, certification, job listings, and products and services.

NWFA: National Wood Flooring Association
16388 Westwoods Business Park
Ellisville, MO 63021
800-422-4556
http://www.woodfloors.org

NWFA represents wood floor installers, manufacturers, distributors, and retailers. It provides up-to-date information and courses on installation, sanding and finishing, and advanced techniques. Its Web site allows you to search contractors, products and suppliers, and features flooring selection and maintenance guidance for contractors and homeowners.

SWRI: Sealant, Waterproofing, & Restoration Institute
2841 Main Street
Kansas City, MO 64108
816-472-SWRI
http://www.swrionline.org

SWRI is a non-profit corporation of contractors, manufacturers, and consultants for the sealant, waterproofing, and restoration industry. The organization promotes industry standards and application techniques and offers technical bulletins, workshops, seminars, and training.

TCA: Tile Council of America
100 Clemson Research Blvd.
Anderson, SC 29625
864-646-8453
http://www.tileusa.com

TCA is a national trade association of tile manufacturers. It develops and patents installation materials and tests tile, setting material, and installation methods. The TCA publishes the *Handbook for Ceramic Tile Installation*, which describes in detail the methods and standards for ceramic tile installation.

WDMA: Window & Door Manufacturers Association
(Formerly National Wood Windows and Doors Association)
1400 E. Touhy Avenue
Suite 470
Des Plaines, IL 60018
800-223-2301
http://www.nwwda.org

WDMA is a trade association that represents manufacturers and suppliers of windows and doors. Its Web site provides information on WDMA standards, technical articles and how-to guides, and product directory.

Codes, Standards, Safety, and Regulatory Agencies

ACI: American Concrete Institute International
P.O. Box 9094
Farmington Hills, MI 48333
248-848-3700
http://www.aci-int.org

ACI produces many publications on the details of correct concrete design and construction, and offers certification and educational opportunities. Most building codes rely on references to ACI for concrete standards.

ADA: The American with Disabilities Act
U.S. Department of Justice
ADA Information Line: 800-514-0301
http://www.usdoj.gov/crt/ada/adahom1.htm

The ADA site offers a free hotline to ask questions about the ADA, as well as information about ADA regulation updates, building code certification, and publications and resources for obtaining ADA standards.

ANSI: American National Standards Institute
1819 L Street, NW
Suite 600
Washington, DC 20036
212-642-4900
http://www.ansi.org

ANSI regulates the nation's standardization for products and workmanship. Many local and state governments and other agencies have adopted ANSI's voluntary standards. ANSI's Web site provides up-to-date information on standards (including a link to purchase electronic copies), and a reference library.

APA: The Engineered Wood Association
(Formerly the American Plywood Association)
Box 11700
Tacoma, WA 98411
253-565-6600
http://www.apawood.org

APA sets standards for quality inspection and testing of wood and offers over 400 publications, technical reports, and market studies with information about engineered wood products. Its Web site offers extensive product and application information, as well as a free downloadable manual for residential and commercial construction, which includes information on topics such as floor, wall, and roof systems; specification practices; quality standards; and fire-rated finishing methods.

ASHRAE: American Society of Heating, Refrigerating, and Air-Conditioning Engineers
1791 Tullie Circle NW
Atlanta, GA 30329
404-636-8400
http://www.ashrae.org

ASHRAE develops standards for uniform methods of testing, rating, and installing HVAC and refrigeration equipment. Its Web site allows you to download standards and guidelines.

ASTM: The American Society for Testing and Materials
100 Barr Harbor Drive
West Conshohocken, PA 19428
610-832-9585
http://www.astm.org

ASTM develops standards based on test methods for materials, products, and practices for building products including metals, paints, and plastics, as well as consumer products and electronics. More than 10,000 ASTM standards are published annually, and many are referenced in building codes and regulations. The ASTM Web site offers up-to-date information (including on-line subscriptions to the society's standards, magazines, and journals); training courses on topics such as testing of roofing, plastics, and corrosion; and quality assurance programs.

BHMA: Builders Hardware Manufacturers Association
355 Lexington Avenue
17th Floor
New York, NY 10017
212-297-2122
http://www.buildershardware.com

BHMA is accredited by the American National Standards Institute (ANSI) to develop hardware performance standards. BHMA member manufacturers produce most of the hardware used for the construction industry, including items such as locks, hinges, cabinet hardware, weatherstripping, and architectural trim. Its Web site provides information on ANSI/BHMA standards, product certification, and links to member companies.

CSI: The Construction Specifications Institute
99 Canal Center Plaza
Suite 300
Alexandria, VA 22314
800-689-2900
http://www.csinet.org

CSI offers technical publications and standards (including its *Manual of Practice*), certification programs, and educational opportunities (including seminars, on-line courses, and continuing education). CSI develops and maintains the MasterFormat®, a widely used system for classifying, specifying, and estimating the elements of a construction project.

ICC: International Code Council
5203 Leesburg Pike
Suite 600
Falls Church, VA 22041
703-931-4533
http://www.intlcode.org

ICC is a code development organization that maintains a family of *International Codes*, including the *International Building Code®* (IBC) and the *International Residential Code®* (IRC). ICC is made up of the three major model code associations, Building Officials and Code Administrators International, Inc. (BOCA), International Conference of Building Officials (ICBO), and Southern Building Code Congress International, Inc. (SBCCI).

NAFC: National Alliance for Fair Contracting
1 North Old State Capitol Plaza
Suite 525
Springfield, IL 62701
866-523-NAFC
http://www.faircontracting.org

NAFC addresses construction employment issues, and provides contractors with updates and training on laws and regulations for fair competitive bidding and construction of public projects.

NFPA: National Fire Protection Association
1 Batterymarch Park
P.O. Box 9101
Quincy, MA 02269
617-770-3000
http://www.nfpa.org

NFPA provides fire, electrical, and life safety codes and standards and maintains the *National Electrical Code®* (NFPA 70) and the *Life Safety Code®* (NFPA 101), among many others. The *Life Safety Code®* sets the minimum design requirements for protection from fire and other emergencies. Many states mandate compliance with this code.

NSC: National Safety Council
1121 Spring Lake Drive
Itasca, IL 60143
800-621-7619
http://www.nsc.org

NSC is a non-government and non-profit organization that tracks and compiles injury and illness data and publishes safety statistics. It provides information on job safety and preventing job-related injuries for the construction and other industries.

OSHA: Occupational Safety & Health Association
U.S. Department of Labor
Office of Public Affairs
Room N3647
200 Constitution Avenue
Washington, DC 20210
202-693-1999
http://www.osha.gov

OSHA oversees and enforces workplace safety and health and tracks job-related injuries and illnesses of over 80,000 high hazard workplaces. OSHA's Web site provides comprehensive information on its requirements, as well as on topics such as scaffolding, dealing with hazardous materials, record keeping, and training. A special section is devoted to small business, and offers free workplace consultations to help establish safety programs and identify hazards.

SIA: Scaffold Industry Association
20335 Ventura Blvd #310
Woodland Hills, CA 91364
818-610-0320
http://www.scaffold.org

SIA represents scaffold dealers and distributors and provides information for contractors. The organization promotes scaffold safety and offers educational seminars and training courses searchable by your state. Its Web site also provides technical articles, code information, and product and distributor listings.

UL: Underwriters Laboratories, Inc.
333 Pfingsten Road
Northbrook, IL 60062
847-272-8800
http://www.ul.com

UL is a product safety testing and certification organization that tests and lists construction systems and components for qualities such as fire- and wind-resistance and has listings for electrical equipment and products. Its Web site offers information on standards, safety, testing, training, and products.

Useful Internet Sites

The following Web sites are just a few examples of Internet resources for builders and remodelers. While some of these companies may offer free services (such as Web sites, e-mail addresses, and marketing opportunities), many may carry associated fees. Please consult the sites for more information.

http://www.thebluebook.com
The Blue Book of Building and Construction provides over 800,000 company listings for all aspects of construction, including information on contractors, subcontractors, material and equipment suppliers, and manufacturers. You can search by your region to locate the information you need, including company profiles. The Blue Book serves as a project management system, allowing you to build lists of your preferred vendors, receive industry updates, manage your bids, set up your project calendar, and send and receive project documents.

http://www.build.com
Build.com offers extensive resources for contractors, service professionals, and homeowners. The Web site offers comprehensive directories of manufacturers of building products and equipment (such as appliances, tools, paint, hardware, etc.) and professional services (building plans, contractor referrals, and business resources). You can find trade publications, new products, and industry news.

http://www.buzzsaw.com
This site offers Web-based resources for building professionals, including project and bid management tools, industry news and information, and directories of materials and equipment resources. Through buzzsaw.com, contractors can manage all aspects of

projects on-line, including design, document organization and development, construction progress, and communication with all other involved parties—customers, architects, engineers, etc.

http://contractor.com

Contractors will find information here on all aspects of the construction business—from product manufacturer information, to educational opportunities, to a contractor referral program with over 800,000 contractors. You can use the site to set up a Web site and market your company, get financial management information (legal advice, payroll services, and tax information), find scheduling and estimating software, pull permits, find house plans, and get documents for your company (such as contracts, employee handbooks, and estimating forms).

http://www.housingzone.com

HousingZone offers resources for builders, remodelers, architects, and suppliers, including industry updates, buyer's guides, and articles. It provides business management tools such as on-line forms, certification and education through the Home Builder's Institute, and information on construction methods, materials, building codes, and legislation. HousingZone is created by the publishers of the magazines *Professional Builder* and *Professional Remodeler*.

Recommended Reading

The following publications are valuable resources for builders and remodelers. They are available at home centers and major book stores, or by calling the publisher, R.S. Means Co., Inc., directly at 1-800-334-3509 or visiting the company's on-line book store at **http:// www.rsmeans.com**

Builder's Essentials: Framing and Rough Carpentry by Scot Simpson. New second edition is an illustrated course on residential and light commercial framing and rough carpentry. Includes professional guidance on framing of walls, floors, stairs, windows, doors, and roofs. Also covers equipment and material handling, safety, and the latest building code requirements. $24.95 ISBN: 0-87629-617-7

Builder's Essentials: Advanced Framing Techniques by Scot Simpson. R.S. Means, Co., Inc. Provides an advanced course for challenging framing projects, and includes professional guidance on engineered wood products, wood and steel framing, special building code requirements, and framing of stairs, roofs, windows, and walls. $24.95 ISBN: 0-87629-618-5

Builder's Essentials: Plan Reading & Material Takeoff by Wayne J. DelPico. R.S. Means, Co., Inc. Provides professional guidance on reading and interpreting building plans and performing quantity takeoffs to meet professional standards. Covers all major construction divisions, such as concrete, masonry, and carpentry, and uses plans and tables to illustrate plan reading and takeoff procedures. Over 160 illustrations provide explanation of standards and symbols. $35.95 ISBN: 0-87629-348-8

Contractor's Pricing Guide: Framing & Rough Carpentry. R.S. Means, Co., Inc. This annually updated book provides prices for all aspects of framing and rough carpentry for residential and light commercial construction. Costs are easily adjusted to your location. The book also includes forms, graphics, and charts for accurate estimating. $36.95 ISBN: 0-87629-601-0

Contractor's Pricing Guide: Residential Detailed Costs. R.S. Means, Co., Inc. Covers all aspects of residential construction, from overhead costs and productivity, to wiring, lighting, and more. Helps you accurately estimate the cost of work, including labor and equipment. $36.95 ISBN: 0-87629-599-5

Contractor's Pricing Guide: Residential Square Foot Costs. R.S. Means, Co., Inc. A professional guide to planning and budgeting the cost of new homes. Contains over 250 residences of different sizes and types. Allows you to build your own costs or modify model costs to meet your project elements. $39.95 ISBN: 0-87629-600-2

Exterior Home Improvement Costs. R.S. Means, Co., Inc. Estimates for 64 projects, including room additions and garages, decks, paving and patios, painting and siding, windows and doors, fences and landscaping. $19.95 ISBN: 0-87629-575-8

Interior Home Improvement Costs. R.S. Means, Co., Inc. Estimates for 66 projects, including kitchen and bath remodeling, home offices, attic and basement conversions, fireplaces, lighting, security systems, and more. $19.95 ISBN: 0-87629-576-6

Residential & Light Commercial Construction Standards. R.S. Means, Co., Inc. A one-stop reference for authoritative information on quality standards, overviews of installation methods, and common defect items to watch out for in new construction or remodeling—from paving, concrete and masonry, to framing, finish work and cabinetry, doors and windows, roofing, painting and wallpapering, and HVAC/plumbing/electrical. $59.95 ISBN: 0-87629-499-9

Historic Preservation: Project Planning & Estimating. R.S. Means, Co., Inc. Expert guidance on managing historic restoration, rehabilitation, and preservation building projects and determining and controlling their costs. This comprehensive resource includes information on building codes and standards, site survey and documentation, protecting finishes and features, finding specialty subcontractors, and how to evaluate and repair over 75 historic building materials. $99.95 ISBN: 0-87629-573-1

Glossary

Arbitration

Resolving disputes by submitting the conflict to an unbiased third party for review. Arbitration is a less expensive alternative to court proceedings, and its results are binding. For non-binding dispute resolution, see *mediation*.

As-Built drawings

Drawings made during construction that record the location, size, and nature of concealed items such as structural elements, accessories, equipment, devices, plumbing, mechanical equipment, etc. Also referred to as *record drawings*.

Backcharge

Charging a party with whom you have an agreement (such as a subcontractor or supplier) for their nonperformance by deducting that amount from the payment you would have made for him. For example, if a subcontractor fails to perform a part of the agreement, you may reserve the right to backcharge him for the cost associated with having to complete the work for him.

Bid

A complete, signed proposal to perform designated work for a stipulated sum. See also *proposal*.

Bilateral change clause

Requires both parties (owner and contractor) to agree on a change and its price before work begins on the change. See also *unilateral change clause* and *construction change directive*.

Budget

An itemized estimate of the value of a portion of, or total cost of, a construction project. Also the amount expected to be spent over a given period of time.

Business plan

Your company's plan (measures to be taken and associated cost) for achieving the goals set forth in the strategic plan.

Cash flow management

Managing your money so that you retain as much money as possible within the company, while having cash available to pay bills.

Change order

Written authorization approving a change from the original plans, specifications, or other contract documents. With proper signatures, a change order is considered a legal document.

Construction change directive

Directive that allows the owner to direct the contractor to perform work that is different from that presented in the contract. Includes the owner's estimate of the work. Also referred to as *constructive change*. See also *bilateral* and *unilateral change clause*.

Construction management fee only contract

Contract specifying payment based on supervision of subcontractors only. This type of contract may be used if the contractor's only responsibility is to oversee and direct the activities of others.

Content conflict

Conflict resulting from a dispute over project elements, such as quality of materials. Content conflicts may be resolved by talking over the matter, or consulting a mediator for an unbiased opinion. See also *relationship conflict*.

Contract

A binding agreement between two parties to perform work on a construction project. See also *contract documents*.

Contract documents

All of the written and graphic documents concerning execution of a particular construction contract. These include the agreement between the owner and the contractor, all conditions of the contract, the specifications and drawings, any changes, and other relevant documents.

Cost plus a fixed fee
Payment based on the actual costs associated with performing the work of a construction project plus a negotiated flat fee (which may be a fixed amount or a percentage of costs).

Direct costs
Costs related to field production and employees, including materials, tools, equipment, subcontractors, permits, and insurance. These must be priced project-to-project and reflected in the contract price.

Estimate
The anticipated cost of materials, labor, and equipment necessary to perform the work required for a project. Estimates should also account for profit and expenses, such as overhead, insurance, testing and inspections, and time- or weather-sensitive costs. See also *unit price estimate*.

Excusable delays
A delay to contract performance that is beyond the control and is not the fault of the contractor. Excusable delays may include unforeseeable weather conditions or owner changes.

Final inspection
A walk-through inspection of a completed project to ensure that the work conforms to the design and contract documents.

Fixed costs
Overhead costs that remain the same for running your business, such as mortgage payments for a home office. These must be paid whether or not you have revenue coming in. Also called *non-variable costs*.

Indirect costs
Overhead or indirect costs incurred by achieving a project's completion, but not applicable to any specific task.

Labor only contract
Contract specifying payment for labor performed only. This type of agreement may be used if the contractor is not responsible for providing the materials.

Lien

A legal means of establishing or giving notice of a claim or an unsatisfied charge in the form of a debt, obligation, or duty. Liens may be filed with the government against property titles, and must be satisfied or adjudicated before the title can be transferred.

Liquidated damages

An amount specified in the contract to cover damages incurred by the owner as a result of the contractor's failure to complete the work within the time frame set forth. The amount should not be a penalty and should be directly related to expenses such as additional time required for an architect, delay of occupancy, or lodging, transportation, or storage costs.

Litigation

Resolving disputes by submitting the conflict to a jurisdiction and the procedures of state or federal courts.

Lump sum contract

Contract that specifies the total payment for performance of the work.

Mediation

Resolving disputes by consulting an objective third party (mediator), whose job it is to quickly resolve differences without resorting to arbitration or litigation. The involved parties come to an agreement themselves, rather than having a decision imposed on them. See also *arbitration* and *litigation*.

Overhead

The cost of running your business and home office other than direct job costs. Overhead costs may include computer and office supplies, accounting and administrative personnel, payment of interest on debt, and insurance.

PPOIC

Acronym for People, Planning, Organization, Implementation, and Control. These represent the most important components to a business that require careful management attention.

Proactive management

Anticipating hazards and problems before they occur. Proactive management includes things like assessing risks, planning for the company's future, staying up-to-date on trends and industry advancements, and enforcing quality standards.

Proposal

A written statement given to the owner that sets forth an offer to perform the work on a project (including all labor, materials, and equipment) for a specified price. See also *bid*.

Punch list

A list of items identified during the final inspection that remain to be completed or corrected to bring the project into compliance with the expectations described in the contract documents at the time of substantial completion.

Quality assurance

A plan for assuring that expected levels of quality are met. QA involves setting standards, policies, and procedures to make sure a project runs smoothly and meets quality requirements.

Quality control

A system of monitoring the quality of the work involved in a project. QC includes inspection of work and materials, overseeing work of crew and subcontractors, keeping records of construction steps, and getting customer feedback.

Relationship conflict

Conflicts that go beyond project specifics to escalate to personal insults. Relationship conflicts should be avoided, as they can cost money and damage reputations. See also *content conflicts*.

Request for information (RFI)

A written request to the owner or architect for information about elements of the contract documents.

Request for proposal (RFP)

A written request to an involved party (subcontractor, architect, etc.) for a proposal or estimate.

Revenue forecast

Your company's anticipated earnings based on consideration of work already in progress and planned work.

Risk management

Attempting to reduce financial, safety, or other potential risks that could bring about loss in the process of construction.

Schedule

A chronological itemization, often in chart form, of the sequence of project tasks involved in completing a construction project.

Scope of work

Statement within the contract documents that describes in detail the work involved in the project, including the quantity and quality of materials, responsibilities of each party, and when work will be performed. Plans and specifications are part of the scope of work.

Site visit

A complete examination of a job site and its conditions done before assembling a bid on a project. Multiple visits may be required to thoroughly investigate and document existing conditions, concealed conditions, and potential risks.

Square foot estimate

Estimated cost per square foot based on the proposed size and use of a space and specific project elements. Often broken down into different construction components.

Strategic plan

A company's future goals, also called a *market plan*. A strategic plan should address what market you want to be in, what level of growth you want to attain each year, and what other goals you plan to achieve.

Subcontract

An agreement between a contractor and subcontractor (specializing in a particular trade) for the completion of a portion of work which the subcontractor will perform, and for which the contractor is responsible.

Submittal

A product or material sample, manufacturer's data, shop drawing, or other such item submitted to the owner or architect by the contractor or subcontractors for the purpose of approval or selection or other action, usually a requirement of the contract documents.

Substantial completion

The condition of the work when the project is ready for owner occupancy and acceptance. Any items that remain to be completed should be duly noted or stipulated in writing.

Unilateral change clause

Grants the owner the sole right to order a change, even if other involved parties do not agree whose responsibility it is or on the price. See also *bilateral change clause* and *construction change directive*.

Unit price

Current and accurate cost of materials, equipment, and labor for one unit (e.g., square foot or each) of a particular construction item. The unit price is multiplied by the appropriate quantity to obtain the total cost for that component of the job. A unit price contract specifies the price per unit for materials and/or services. See also *unit price estimate*.

Unit price estimate

An accurate and detailed estimate that specifies as closely as possible the anticipated costs of the project, including materials, labor, and equipment.

Index

Crisis Control... Dealing with Emergency Situations

☛ **Problem: You've run your credit line out.**

Ways to deal with it:

- Talk with your creditors and ask for additional credit. (This usually works if your credit history is good and if the term is short.)
- Explain to suppliers and vendors that you may need a little additional time. Again, if your history and reputation are good, most suppliers are apt to be agreeable.
- Talk with clients who are late or slow payers, and explain the necessity of timely payments.

Ways to avoid this in the future:

Make sure your contracts with customers provide for interest on late payments. This usually deters clients from paying late. Project your cash flow on projects that require extra capital, and discuss the peak period with your bank or lender ahead of time so that they are aware you may need an extension on your credit line during these peak periods. Above all, never avoid the problem. Suppliers become very reluctant to deal with a contractor that they have had to chase for months.

☛ **Problem: A customer plans to sue you.**

Ways to deal with it:

- Maintain a dialogue with the client. When everyone talks, problems can be avoided or resolved before they become full-blown disasters.
- It is always best to try to reason with the client to avoid taking a matter to court. Once a legal battle has begun in earnest, it is difficult to turn back. Money has been spent on lawyers and everyone wants satisfaction.
- If a legal battle is unavoidable, the best advice is to contact a lawyer.

Ways to avoid this in the future:

Almost all contractors will face a legal problem at least once in their career. It is best to have a lawyer selected ahead of time, rather than trying to interview and retain one at the last minute. Knowing one in advance is helpful if all that is needed is some advice. Attorneys are like doctors; they specialize, so the selection process can take some time. Ask around, talk with other people you respect, and find out who specializes in construction-related law.

☛ **Problem: A crew member quits halfway through a big job, leaving you strapped and needing someone right away.**

Ways to deal with it:

- Call a friendly competitor and ask to borrow an employee. This may include the competitor adding profit and overhead to the employee's salary.
- If the economy is strong and a competitor can't spare an employee, contact the local suppliers you do business with (e.g., lumberyard or supply house) and ask if they know of anyone who is not busy or may be looking for work.
- Work the remaining crew a couple of additional hours each day (or work weekends) until the crisis is manageable.

Ways to avoid this in the future:

Unfortunately, there are no sure-fire ways to prevent losing employees at busy times. The best way to minimize delays is to maintain a network of tradespeople. Stay in touch with good, former employees; maintain relationships through local business associations; and above all, maintain a reputation as a fair and reasonable employer. Good news travels!

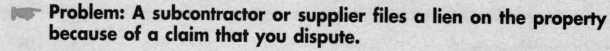

☞ **Problem: A subcontractor or supplier files a lien on the property because of a claim that you dispute.**

Ways to deal with it:

- Always try to negotiate, not litigate.
- Call your attorney, and call the customer and explain the circumstances so he doesn't think you are at fault. Let him know you will see to it that he gets a clear title.
- Contact the subcontractor or supplier and try to find a way to solve the problem without putting a lien on the client's property.
- Compile your documentation and try to negotiate as soon as possible to resolve the problem amicably.
- Use a mediator if you can't settle through negotating. But if you owe it, pay it!

Ways to avoid this in the future:

Make sure the payment schedule you set up in your contract with your customer will enable you to pay subcontractors and suppliers on time.

Maintain thorough files and keep everything written down to avoid disputes. You should keep records of all communications, invoices, check numbers, etc.

☞ **Problem: A customer refuses to pay for extras that he said he wanted, but never documented. The amount is significant.**

Ways to deal with it:

- Check your meeting notes and daily reports to see if there is a record of the customer directing the extra work.
- Get written statements from your employees and subs.
- Show on original drawings that the extra work was not a part of the contract. (Your as-built drawings should highlight the changes.)
- Document extra costs using daily records, invoices, time sheets, and photographs.
- With this information, try to work things out amicably.
- If you are justified, and the client clearly owes you this amount, exercise your rights. (Be aware that your lien rights expire at some point.)

Ways to avoid this in the future:

AVO: Avoid Verbal Orders. Extras should be incorporated into the contract by a written and signed change order to protect you and the customer.

Keep documentation of all changes and directives. Keep thorough logs and updated drawings that track all changes.

Crisis Control... Dealing with Emergency Situations

 Problem: You discover hazardous material on the site during construction.

Ways to deal with it:

- Stop work.
- Contact the architect and customer, and appropriate government agency.
- Check the plans to see if the material was disclosed in the contract documents.
- Determine what needs to happen to solve the problem. (Consult the Board of Health and building officials.)
- Work with the client and architect to put together a plan and costs before proceeding.
- Follow the approved remediation plan exactly as specified.
- Keep track of costs on a time and material basis, and document and photograph the work that you do.
- Request that the architect/engineer or government agency sign off.

Ways to avoid this in the future:

Make sure you are educated and kept up to date on hazardous materials that may be encountered in the type of work you do. Know what to look for, and keep records of who to contact.

Conduct thorough site investigations before submitting a bid so that concealed conditions and potential risks are discussed in advance.

If you suspect that testing (e.g., soils test) is necessary, always discuss the situation with the owner and get written approval for the extra cost.

 Problem: About halfway through the project, it appears that there will be substantial cost and schedule overruns.

Ways to deal with it:

- Address the situation right away, while there is still time to try to get back on track.
- Determine if there are any authorized extras that have not yet been billed.
- Find out if there are delays due to customer decision-making or caused by subs for which there are no backcharges.
- Prepare a revised schedule with the additional costs needed to complete the project.
- Look for opportunities to improve both areas.
- Review job planning and supervision, and let the customer know about the situation.
- Inform the lending institution (if there is one).
- Don't skimp on materials or workmanship to try to save money – this often costs you more in the long run.

Ways to avoid this in the future:

Establish a plan and policies for avoiding cost and schedule overruns, so that if they occur again in the future, you have a system to deal with them quickly.

In your contracts, provide provisions for changes and unforeseen delays. Review your estimating method to make sure your estimates are as accurate as possible.

Crisis Control... Dealing with Emergency Situations

☞ **Problem: After construction is complete, your customer complains of a roof or window leak.**

Ways to deal with it:

- Respond immediately!
- Investigate the problem and determine if it is the subcontractor, manufacturer, or your own employees who need to solve the problem.
- Notify all relevant insurance companies in writing.
- Put a plan together quickly to fix the leak (a real fix – not a band-aid). Water damage occurs slowly, but the ultimate damage to materials and inside furnishings can be substantial.

Ways to avoid this in the future:

Purchase only from established manufacturers with a quality reputation and appropriate warranties. Ask the manufacturer or supplier about problems that may be anticipated if their products are used in your project's circumstances. Make sure subs and your own employees are properly trained in the required installation methods.

☞ **Problem: During the demolition phase of a project, a condition is discovered that was previously concealed and is now going to increase the cost of work.**

Ways to deal with it:

- Discovering a concealed problem in renovation work is a fairly common occurrence and should come as no shock to the client. Most contracts have a provision for just such an event.
- Contact the client and/or the architect immediately. Describe the problem, the solution, and the extra cost, so that they can provide the appropriate direction to you. At the very least, make the client aware of the problem. If the client agrees with your solution and the extra work, have him sign off on it and proceed with the work. Builders who proceed to correct concealed conditions without being directed to do so may end up doing so for free.
- Document the situation carefully, including taking photographs.

Ways to avoid this in the future:

This is a situation that cannot be avoided in remodeling work. The best way to protect yourself against "getting stuck" is to provide for this condition in the contract. The most widely used contracts have specific language dealing with concealed conditions and the need to document, document, document!

Make sure your contracts state who is responsible for costs associated with concealed conditions, and the impact they will have on the project.

Best Solutions to Common Problems

Problem: The weather doesn't cooperate with the task at hand.

Ways to deal with it:

Unfortunately, the weather is an uncontrollable factor in the construction industry. You have two choices (and either may be expensive):

- Roll with the punches and wait out the weather, or
- Spend the money to enclose and/or control the temperature or humidity on the project to keep the work going.
- If necessary, notify the customer and ask for a time extension. (If you have an excusable delay clause in your contract, you may be justified if the weather conditions were unforeseeable.)

Ways to avoid this in the future:

Always follow the weather reports, especially if the project is weather-sensitive. With the exception of sudden weather changes, most weather is forecast over several days and work can be planned around it. Schedule weather-sensitive tasks within appropriate seasons, even if it means doing them out of sequence.

In your contract, include conditions for unforeseeable weather situations.

Problem: You install a product and it turns out to be defective.

Ways to deal with it:

- Identify and document the cause of the failure if possible. Documentation may include taking pictures.
- Call the distributor's or manufacturer's representative to have someone look at the problem and provide their opinion. If the product is defective, ask the manufacturer or distributor what level of responsibility they are going to assume, and get it in writing.
- Keep the owners informed. Let them know how the situation will be handled. Honesty is the best policy.

Ways to avoid this in the future:

Always install a product in accordance with the manufacturer's instructions to prevent the warranty from being voided. If you are not familiar with the product, learn how to install it beforehand. Most manufacturers provide literature, installation instructions, or even videos on how to install the product. A few minutes of reading or instruction now could save a lot of money later.

Problem: Your job gets rained out one afternoon. Should the crew be paid for a full day?

Ways to deal with it:

- Most contractors have a policy for just such a circumstance. Make sure the crew is aware of your policy when you hire them.
- Keep in mind that if you don't already have a policy in place, then whatever you decide on that rainy afternoon will be considered policy going forward. Careful consideration should be given to anything that can be construed as future policy.

Ways to avoid this in the future:

Put a policy in place in writing for all new hires. Most tradespeople are hourly wage personnel and expect to be paid only for the time that they are working. Common sense should prevail, however. If the rain occurs 15 minutes before the end of the day, you can pay them through the end of the day as a gesture of goodwill and expect the time to be made up at a later date. Some contractors have an established policy that if they are rained out on a weekday, they work the crew on Saturday in order to allow the hourly personnel to make up the time. Whatever the policy, stick to it.

Best Solutions to Common Problems

☞ **Problem: Your framing subcontractor fails to adequately staff the job and doesn't keep up with the schedule.**

Ways to deal with it:

- Meet with the subcontractor to determine whether he is capable of and has the resources to perform the work. If so, work with him to get him back on schedule. Termination for default is an extreme measure and should be used only when absolutely justified and necessary.
- If necessary, come up with a recovery plan to find good replacement subs and get the job back on track.

Ways to avoid this in the future:

Make sure you have an agreed upon and realistic schedule as part of your agreement with subcontractors. Get in the habit of writing letters to subs to inform them when to mobilize, and document any delinquencies. Give written notice to "cure" defaults within the time specified in the contract. Absolutely follow the terms of the contract, and the performance bond if there is one. Maintain daily records that show subs' performance and staffing history.

☞ **Problem: Defective materials are delivered to the site, which may delay the project.**

Ways to deal with it:

- Give the supplier written and oral notification of the defects immediately.
- Make arrangements to have the materials removed and replaced as soon as possible.
- Take pictures of the defects if helpful, and protect the materials from further damage while on site.
- Keep track of project costs if the project is delayed.

Ways to avoid this in the future:

Always inspect material deliveries right away so that if there are any defects, the shipment can be replaced quickly to avoid project delays.

Use suppliers you are familiar with—those who provide quality materials, personalized service, and product warranties.

Notes

Notes